OAKWOOD LIBRARY OF RAILWAY HIS'

The ALSTON BRANCH

by

Stanley C. Jenkins MA

THE OAKWOOD PRESS

British Library Cataloguing in Publication Data
A Record for this book is available from the British Library
ISBN 0 85361 574 8

First Edition published 1991
Second Edition 2001

Printed by Inkon Printers Ltd, Yateley, Hants.

Our Kind thanks to J.F. Addyman for his advice and use of structure drawings.

Front cover: Ex-LNER 'J39' class 0-6-0 No. 64814 pulls away from Lambley station with a train for Alston. In the background is the impressive Lambley viaduct. *Colour-Rail*

Rear cover, top: 'J39' No. 64812 stands at Alston having arrived with a special. Just visible in the engine shed is BR Standard class '3' 2-6-0 No. 77014. *Colour-Rail*

Rear cover, below: A class '110' dmu operates the branch passenger service in this view taken near Slaggyford in the line's final years as a standard gauge railway. *Colour-Rail*

Published by The Oakwood Press (Usk), P.O. Box 13, Usk, Mon., NP15 1YS.
E-mail: oakwood-press@dial.pipex.com
Website: www.oakwood-press.dial.pipex.com

Contents

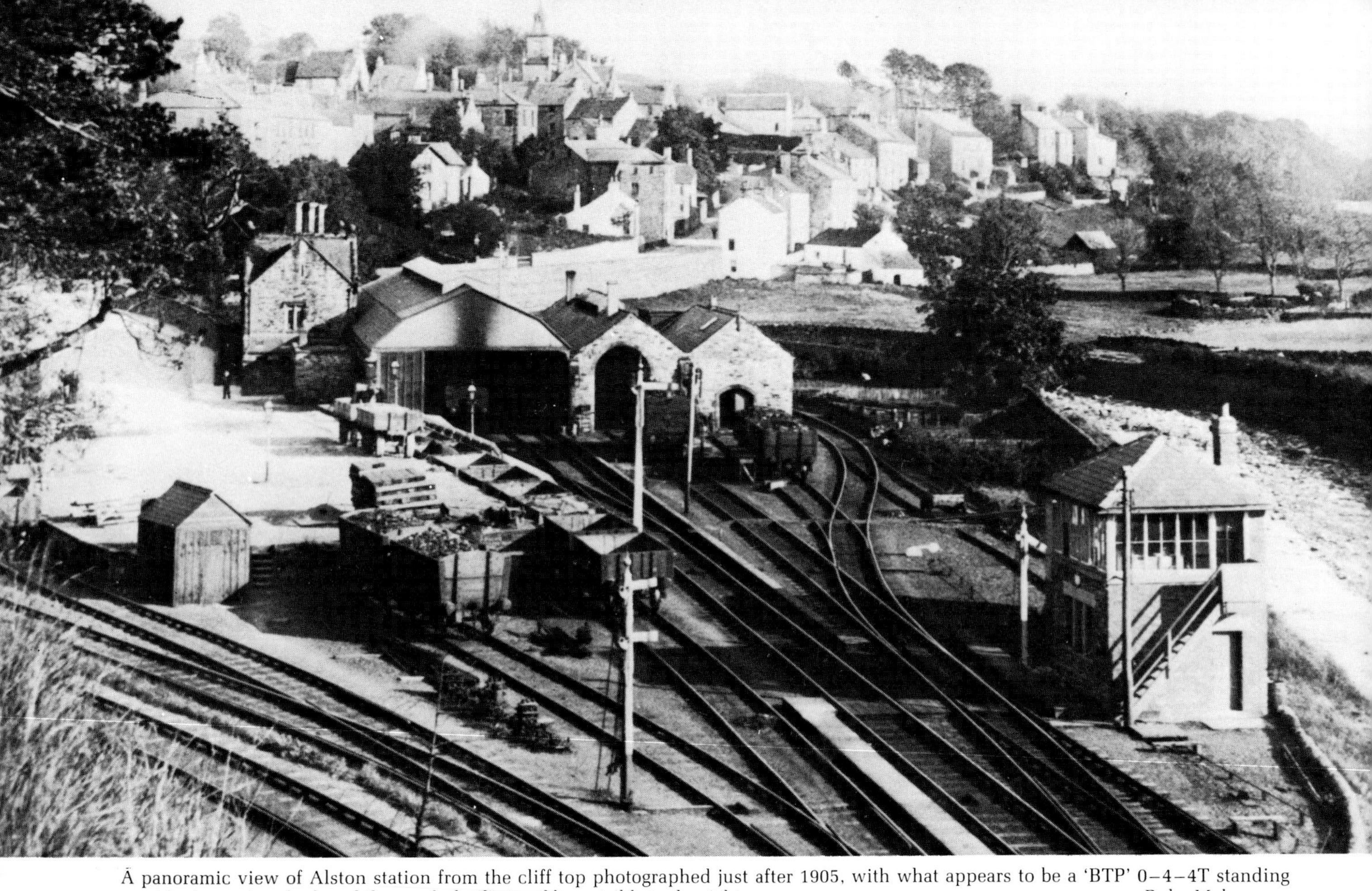

A panoramic view of Alston station from the cliff top photographed just after 1905, with what appears to be a 'BTP' 0–4–4T standing outside the engine shed, and the newly-built signal box visible to the right. *Ruby Makepeace*

Introduction

The railways of the British Isles are, even today, a vast system encompassing a bewildering variety of main lines, cross country routes and branches. Most of these are of interest to railway historians, but some routes are more worthy of study than others, and a few lines have always been firm favourites. The 13¼ mile single track branch from Haltwhistle to Alston was neglected by enthusiasts for many years, but having survived the Beeching closures it belatedly emerged as one of England's best-loved rural lines. It seemed inconceivable that such a line could be closed in its entirety, and when the axe finally fell in 1976, many people regarded the closure as a national tragedy.

The attractions of the Alston line were, perhaps, fourfold; the branch was above all, a highly scenic route serving an area much frequented by hikers and other outdoor enthusiasts, but on top of this inherent advantage it was also a relatively early line, with a long (though straightforward) history dating back to the 1840s. For the enthusiast, the line never became a 'basic' railway, and although it was eventually reduced to one-engine-in-steam operation, much Victorian infrastructure remained intact. Finally, the history of the branch was inextricably linked with the story of lead and coal mining in the Alston Moor area, and although these activities were peripheral to the railway, they add an extra dimension to an already interesting story.

This monograph was originally to have been written by life-long railway enthusiast Paul Lefevre, who had spent many years researching the story and recording the memories of former railwaymen and travellers. Unfortunately, it was not possible for Mr Lefevre to complete his project, and *The Alston Branch* was therefore written by S.C. Jenkins (who had, quite fortuitously, been working on the early history of railways in the north Pennine area, and had already amassed a body of evidence relating to the 1840–62 period). It is hoped that the resulting history will be of value, not only to railway enthusiasts and potential modellers, but also to local historians and to all those with an interest in the South Tynedale region.

Witney, Oxfordshire
1990

Alston, the highest market town in England, as viewed from an old postcard at the turn of the century. *Oakwood Collection*

The station at Alston as seen on a postcard dated 1908. *Oakwood Collection*

Historical Summary

Company of Origin	Newcastle & Carlisle Railway (inc. 22nd May, 1829)
Date of Opening	Haltwhistle–Shaft Hill (goods), March 1851 Alston–Lambley Fell (goods) January 1852 Haltwhistle–Alston (goods and passenger) 17th November, 1852
Date of Closure	1st May, 1976
Length of Branch	13 miles 14 chains
Mode of Operation (1933)	Electric train tablet from Haltwhistle to Coanwood, train staff and ticket from Coanwood to Lambley, and electric train tablet from Lambley to Alston.
Typical Motive Power	Bogie Tank Passenger ('BTP') 0–4–4Ts (later class 'G6'), 'G5' 0–4–4Ts, class 'J21' 0–6–0s, class 'J25' 0–6–0s and class 'J39' 0–6–0s. Also class 'F8' 2–4–2Ts and 'N8' 0–6–2Ts, together with Ivatt class '4MT' 2–6–0s, BR standard class '3MT' 2–6–0s and class '4MT' 2–6–0s.
Acts of Parliament	9 & 10 Vic. cap. 394 (26th August, 1846) — Newcastle & Carlisle Railway (branches). 12 & 13 Vic. cap. 43 (13th July, 1849) — Alston branch deviations.

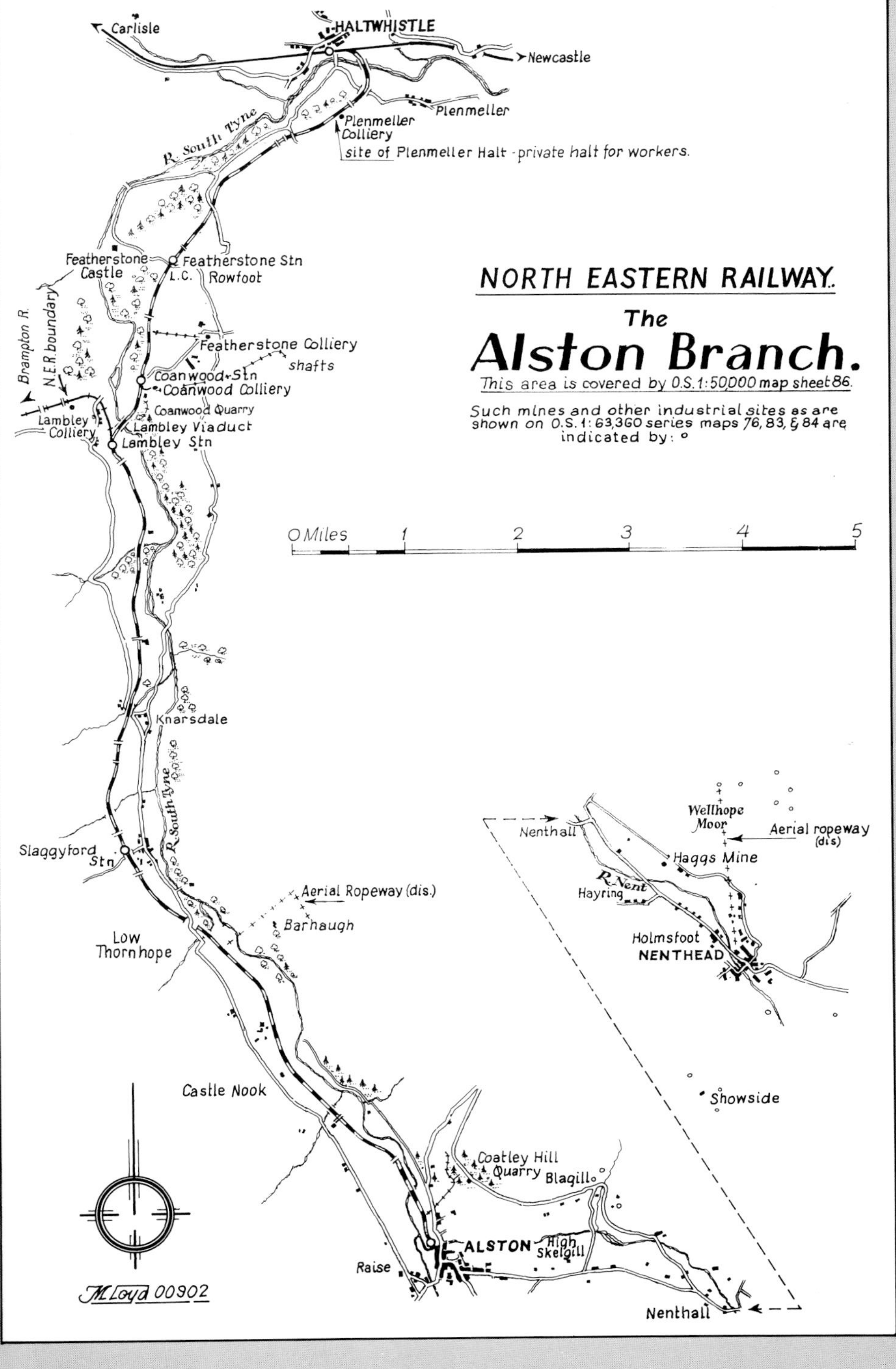
NORTH EASTERN RAILWAY.
The
Alston Branch.
This area is covered by O.S.1:50,000 map sheet 86.
Such mines and other industrial sites as are shown on O.S. 1:63,360 series maps 76, 83, & 84 are indicated by: o
0 Miles 1 2 3 4 5
Carlisle
HALTWHISTLE
Newcastle
Plenmeller
Plenmeller Colliery
site of Plenmeller Halt - private halt for workers.
R. South Tyne
Featherstone Castle
Featherstone Stn
L.C.
Rowfoot
Brampton R.
N.E.R. boundary
Featherstone Colliery
shafts
Coanwood Stn
Coanwood Colliery
Coanwood Quarry
Lambley Colliery
Lambley Viaduct
Lambley Stn
Knarsdale
R. South Tyne
Slaggyford Stn
Aerial Ropeway (dis.)
Barhaugh
Low Thornhope
Castle Nook
Coatley Hill Quarry
Blagill
ALSTON
High Skelgill
Raise
Nenthall
Nenthall
Wellhope Moor
Aerial ropeway (dis)
Haggs Mine
R. Nent
Hayring
Holmsfoot
NENTHEAD
Showside
M Loyd 00902

A double-headed passenger service seen here near Featherstone station with two Alston Branch locomotives working the midday train from Haltwhistle, south to Alston. The Alston locomotive spent most of the time shunting at Haltwhistle and at midday, so that the early and late crews could change shift it had to return to Alston. It was attached to the branch service giving an unusual sight as shown in the photo of a class 'J21' piloting a class 'G5'.

Neville Stead

Chapter One

Origins of the Alston Branch (1800–1862)

Said to be the highest market town in England, Alston is situated in a mountainous district on the borders of Cumbria and Northumberland. Once known as 'Aldeneston', the town is bounded on the west by Hartside Fell (2,046 ft), on the south by Cross Fell (2,930 ft) and on the east by high, rugged lands in the counties of Durham and Northumberland. The town occupies a hillside position at the confluence of the rivers South Tyne and Nent, and its market place is no less than 963 ft above mean sea level.

Alston and the Lead Mining Industry

The origins of Alston are, like those of most English towns, shrouded in mystery; however, the manor was mentioned in an inquest taken in 1315 (after the death of Nicholas de Veteripont) and this early reference tells us much about the area at that time. We are told that the property comprised:

> The capital messuage of Alston, 14 acres of arable land, 100 acres of meadow, 33 tenants of Gerardsgill, with 33 shielings at £5 18*s*. yearly rent; 13 tenants at Amoteshalth at £3 8*s*. 4*d*.; 22 tenants at Nent and Corbrig gate with 22 shielings at 5*s*. 2*d*. yearly rent; also a water corn mill, a fulling mill, and 3,000 acres of pasture in Alston Moor.

This information suggests that Alston was a typical upland-type agricultural community with some 68 households and a population of perhaps 350–400 (assuming around 5 or 6 persons in each cottage). There was no mention of any kind of mining activity at that time, but it is known that lead mining was already an important activity, and contemporary documents contain many references to lead mining in the hills around Alston; in 1417, for example, the 'mine of Alston' was held by William Stapleton at a yearly rent of £10.

In later years, lead mining became of immense importance to the local economy, and there were 119 lead mines in the parish of Alston by 1768; the yearly output of these mines was about 8,000 tons, and the largest mining company was the London Lead Company — a Quaker organisation which leased most of the local mines, and operated a smelter at Nenthead.

In Medieval times, mining had been carried out in a variety of scattered moorland sites, but Alston eventually became the centre of this remote mining area, and by the end of the 18th century Alston and the outlying settlements of Nenthead, Garrigill and Leadgate had become typical mining communities. Minerals found around Alston included, not only lead, but also zinc, copper, sulphur, coal and iron. Lead was, however, the most important source of mineral wealth in the Alston area, and it would be no exaggeration to say that during the first years of the 19th century, Alston was the lead-mining capital of the world. Some idea of the importance of Alston's mines will be apparent from the following table, which shows the average yearly output of the Alston lead mining region, together with figures from comparable mining districts such as Teeside and Weardale. (It should be noted that lead output was traditionally measured in *bings* — a Norse word meaning 'heap'; a bing of lead weighed 8 cwt.)

Table 1

AVERAGE OUTPUT OF LEAD BETWEEN 1800 AND 1825

Mining Areas	*Average Annual Output*
Alston Moor and Cross Fell	19,000 bings
Weardale	17,000 bings
Teesdale	8,000 bings
Allendale	8,000 bings

Like other mining communities, the Alston region was a largely self-contained area, and its miners were a proud and distinct social group. Many of them were non-conformists, and a 19th century writer was impressed by their thrift, sobriety and capacity for hard work:

> I prosecuted a pretty extensive house-to-house visitation, found everything clean, whole, and in its place; no trumpery little ornaments, as in the collier cottages. Where there is a picture, it is that of some favourite minister, such as Wesley; or a copy of the 'Cottar's Saturday Night'. There are in almost every cottage some select Sunday books, besides the Bible and hymn books published by Fullarton, Black or Blackie. I counted 19 copies of the Imperial Dictionary. There were no cheap periodicals or people's editions — they are not reckoned at all canny. The miners like everything good of their kind. Many of them have cows, and not a few of them have a pony also. The remarkable personal beauty of the children as compared with those of the adjoining colliery districts is, I presume, to be attributed to nothing but the transmitted and reflected intelligence, which has resulted to their parents from their moral and religious cultivation. I saw nothing of a neglected brat; no dirty or undarned stockings; no unblackened clogs or unwashed faces. The general character of the lead miners presents a striking contrast to that of the colliers. They consist of families who have lived for ages on the spot . . . a steady, provident, orderly, and industrious people.

These sturdy, upright, Alston lead miners were clearly imbued with the traditional Protestant virtues, but Alston itself could be a depressing place. William Hutchinson, the Cumberland topographer, described the town in less than flattering terms:

> Alston is a small market town, meanly built, situated at a declivity of a steep hill, inhabited by miners. The fatigue of passing bad roads was in no wise alleviated by the scene which presented itself here. Pent in a narrow valley, over which the mountains frowned with a melancholy sterility and nakedness; the wind tempestuous, impending clouds stretching forth a dark and disconsolate curtain over the face of the morning, rain beating vehemently against the windows, which were not able to resist the storm; a few trees standing near the inn tossed by the heavy blasts which howled down the valley; such were the objects which presented themselves to us at Aldston . . . We might be bold to challenge Derbyshire or even Cornwall to produce so peculiarly wild a spot as Aldston Moor; where all that earth produces is from its bowels, and where the people also are so generally subterraneous.

Hutchinson's description (which dates from the late 18th century) underlines the isolation and utter remoteness of pre-railway Alston — an isolation which was, by the late 1700s, posing a very real threat to the continued prosperity of companies such as the London Lead Company. Rivers and canals were the freight arteries of pre-railway Britain, but Alston's mountainous position was hardly conducive to the development of a viable canal system, and in these circumstances teams of ponies were used to transport lead ore from the mines to the smelters. In general, each of these pony teams (or 'galloways') could transport about 2 tons of ore, though in winter the pack horse trails often became impassable.

An Early Scheme

Road construction schemes offered a partial solution to Alston's transport problems, and for this reason the London Lead Company and the Greenwich Hospital (which owned the estate) were keen to build new roads in the area. In 1823 an Act of Parliament was obtained for the building of new roads from the town of Alston to Penrith, Brampton and Hexham, while a further road was subsequently made from Alston to Greta Bridge in neighbouring Yorkshire. These improved road links did much to alleviate Alston's chronic transport difficulties, but the problems posed by winter snowfalls remained, and in this context railway or tramway construction offered an even better solution.

The links between mines and early railways are well-recorded, and it comes as no surprise to discover that a horse-worked railway was in operation in east Cumberland by 1800. This pioneer line served the Earl of Carlisle's collieries at Tindale Fell (to the north west of Alston) and the first

Lambley station photographed in the late Victorian period; the bearded patriarch standing on the platform is possibly station master Henry Laing, whose tenure of office was *c*.1885–95. Note the slotted-post NER signals for the junction.

Lens of Sutton

section — from Tarnhouse Colliery to Brampton — was ceremonially opened on 15th April, 1799. The line was about five miles long, and its gauge was probably less than 4 ft 8 in. The original line was laid with primitive wooden rails, but iron rails had been introduced by 1808; by that time the tramway had been extended to serve neighbouring collieries. Later still, on 9th December, 1828, the route was extended eastwards to serve a colliery at Midgeholme (near Lambley). The Midgeholme branch was a 4 ft 8½ in. gauge line from its inception, and the earlier parts of the system were later converted to this same gauge. Subsequent extensions and improvements resulted in the creation of an extensive system of railways and tramways in the Brampton coal mining area, and by the 1830s George Howard, the sixth Earl of Carlisle, and his agents were actively considering the introduction of locomotive power.

The Earl of Carlisle's colliery railway formed a viable nucleus for future railway development in the Alston area, but in the event this pioneer line was overshadowed by the building of the Newcastle & Carlisle Railway — a much larger undertaking which crossed England from east to west and severed the Tindale Fell tramway at Milton, near Brampton.

Opening of the Newcastle & Carlisle Railway

A very early railway, the Newcastle & Carlisle Company was authorised on 22nd May, 1829 when a group of landowners and entrepreneurs obtained 'An Act for making and maintaining a Railway or Tramroad from the Town of Newcastle-upon-Tyne in the County of the Town of Newcastle-upon-Tyne, to the City of Carlisle, in the County of Cumberland, with a branch thereout'. Capital of £300,000 was rapidly subscribed, and the first section of line was opened on 9th March, 1835, when trains commenced running between Blaydon and Hexham, a distance of twelve miles.

The Newcastle & Carlisle Act prohibited the use of locomotives, but the N&C proprietors realised that their completed line would be far too long for horse operation, and the Blaydon to Hexham line was therefore worked by locomotives from its inception. Unfortunately, a local landowner objected to the use of steam power, and on 28th March the company was obliged to suspend operations on the new railway. Services resumed on 6th May, and on 17th June, 1835 the Newcastle & Carlisle promoters obtained a new Act permitting the use of locomotive power. Further sections of the line were, by that time, nearing completion, and on 11th June, 1836 the route was extended eastwards from Blaydon to the River Derwent; a few days later, on 28th June, the line was pushed westwards from Hexham to Haydon Bridge.

Meanwhile, further progress had been made at the Carlisle end of the route, and on 9th July, 1836 a detached portion of the line was brought into use between Carlisle and Blenkinsopp Colliery, near Haltwhistle. This westernmost section of the N&C main line impinged on the Tindale Fell tramway but, in an attempt to turn the situation to his own advantage, the Earl of Carlisle rebuilt his own line on a new alignment between Brampton and Hallbankgate, with a connection with the Newcastle & Carlisle line at Milton (later Brampton Junction). Henceforth the Earl of Carlisle's tramways

— generally known as The Brampton Railway — employed locomotives for freight operation though, perversely, a horse-drawn 'dandy' was used to convey passengers between Brampton and Brampton Junction! On a foot-note, it is interesting to note that in 1837 Stephenson's historic *Rocket* was purchased for further use on the Brampton line.

The eastern and western sections of the Newcastle & Carlisle route were physically joined on 18th June, 1838 when an eleven mile link was opened between Haydon Bridge and Blenkinsopp Colliery, and on 21st October, 1839 a further extension was opened from Blaydon to Newcastle via Scotswood.

The completed Newcastle & Carlisle line was, in 1838, the longest railway in Britain, the distance from its then terminus at Gateshead to Carlisle being 60 miles; it was also the first railway to cross England from east to west while, on a minor note, the line was unusual in that its trains kept to the right on double track sections! Also of interest is the fact that Thomas Edmondson, 'The inventor of the railway ticket', devised his familiar card ticket system while employed as a booking clerk by the Newcastle & Carlisle company. Hitherto the Newcastle & Carlisle (and other early lines) had relied on a time-consuming book-keeping system that was more suited to the stage coach era than that machine age, but Edmondson's standardised pasteboard tickets revolutionised railway accounting, and 'Edmondson' tickets are today used all over the world (though sadly, BR and Northern Ireland Railways have now abandoned the Edmondson system).

The completion of the Newcastle & Carlisle Railway was of limited use to Alston residents because the nearest station was at Haltwhistle, some twelve miles to the north. Nevertheless, the newly-opened line was welcomed by lead producers who were able to send ore by road to Haltwhistle or Hexham, and thence by rail to the outside world; indeed, the London Lead Company claimed that by using local railways it was able to save up to £800 per year in terms of transportation costs. The Brampton Railway, meanwhile, continued to provide useful transport facilities for nearby coal and limestone producers in the Midgeholme and Tindale Fell areas, and although there was as yet no direct rail link between Alston and the outside world, the presence of these railways ensured that, by 1840, the people of this remote Pennine town were no longer as isolated as they had been in the pack horse era.

Origins of the Alston Line

Although the Brampton Railway and its branches provided a useful transport facility, there was clearly scope for further railway development in the Alston area, and in the 1840s the Newcastle & Carlisle Railway suggested that a branch line might be built along the picturesque South Tyne Valley from Haltwhistle to Alston. Such a line would be of great benefit to local mining companies such as the London Lead Company, and the N&C Directors clearly hoped that substantial coal and lead traffic would develop once the railway was in operation. A modest passenger business was also envisaged, although the remote, underpopulated region through which the railway would run suggested that passenger traffic would always be subordinate to goods and minerals.

A Bill seeking consent for 'The Newcastle-upon-Tyne and Carlisle Railway Company to extend their railway in Newcastle-upon-Tyne, to make several branch railways, and for other purposes connected with their undertaking' was prepared for the 1846 Parliamentary session, and despite sustained (and sometimes bitter) opposition from local farmers and landowners, the N&C scheme successfully passed through the Lower House.

Interestingly, the Newcastle & Carlisle Railway was not alone in seeking to bring rail communication to Alston and Nenthead. Another scheme, known as the Wear Valley Extension Railway, had been laid before Parliament by Quaker interests and although this project did not succeed it would be worth sketching-in some details of the proposed Wear Valley Extension route. It was envisaged that the line would run from a junction with the Newcastle & Carlisle main line at 'Milton' (i.e. the present Brampton station), and, passing through Lambley, it would then follow the South Tyne towards Alston. From Alston, the proposed WVER route was similar to that suggested by the Newcastle & Carlisle Railway — both lines would have passed around the town to reach the Nent Valley, but whereas the N&C Directors intended to terminate their line at Nenthead, the Wear Valley Extension route pressed on boldly through the hills. The gradients between Alston and Nenthead would have been about 1 in 55, and in order to avoid even steeper sections the WVER extension engineers proposed a 2 mile 506 yard tunnel, followed by stretches of 70 ft cuttings and 45 ft embankments on the descent to Wearhead.

If completed, the Wear Valley Extension line would have formed part of a through route between Carlisle, Alston, Wearhead and Darlington, but in reality the WVER scheme was hardly a practicable option. The chosen route would have been prohibitively expensive, and in any case the 34 mile-long Wear Valley Extension line would have been plagued by a succession of adverse gradients on the long climb over Kilhope summit.

The rival Newcastle & Carlisle branch was, in contrast, an entirely feasible project, and as the complex Parliamentary process neared its conclusion, there seemed no reason why the N&C scheme should not be authorised. The proposed 17 mile branch from Haltwhistle to Nenthead would itself necessitate some considerable feats of civil engineering, but it was clear, by the summer of 1846, that the Bill would be successful, and on 26th August, 1846 the Newcastle & Carlisle scheme received the Royal Assent.

The resulting Act (9 & 10 Vic. cap. 394) enabled the Newcastle & Carlisle Railway to extend its existing line and make various new branches, one of which would be the Haltwhistle to Alston line. The authorised route ran from the N&C main line at Haltwhistle to Alston and thence to Nenthead, passing *en route* through the Northumberland townships of Bellister, Featherstone, Lambley and Asholme, Knaresdale and Kirkhaugh. The proposed line followed the South Tyne valley for much of its length, while at Haltwhistle the junction would face towards Newcastle. To pay for these new works, the N&CR was authorised to raise £240,000 in shares and £80,000 by loans.

Unfortunately, an unexpected failure of the potato crop at the end of 1845 sparked off a major economic crisis, and when, in the following year, both the corn and potato harvests failed, the Victorian financial system was thrown into confusion. Poor harvests in 1848 and 1849 led to riots and revolutions throughout Europe, and in these grave and unhappy circumstances the railway stock market collapsed. In common with other railway companies, the Newcastle & Carlisle Railway suffered severely during the crisis years of the late 1840s, and having obtained Parliamentary consent for a branch to Alston and Nenthead, the company was unable to begin construction.

A Further Application to Parliament

In the meantime, the Newcastle & Carlisle Directors had reconsidered their original proposals, and faced with continued opposition from certain landowners at Alston and elsewhere, the N&C Board decided that the scheme would be revised. Over 6½ miles of deviations were proposed, while at Haltwhistle the east-facing junction would be replaced by a junction facing Carlisle. Further changes were anticipated at the Alston end of the route, where the authorised terminus at Nenthead would be abandoned — making Alston the end of the line.

Plans and sections of the proposed deviations were deposited with the clerks of the Peace of the Counties of Northumberland and Cumberland, while further copies were sent to the relevant authorities in Lambley, Alston and neighbouring parishes 'on or before the thirtieth day of November' 1848. Detailed notices were also placed in local newspapers, under the heading 'Alterations of, and Branch from Alston Branch'. These notices explained that:

> Application is to be made to Parliament in the ensuing session for an Act to alter, amend, and enlarge the Powers and Provisions of an Act passed in the session held in the Ninth and Tenth years of the Reign of her present Majesty Queen Victoria, intituled 'An Act to authorise the Newcastle-upon-Tyne and Carlisle Railway Company to extend their Railway in Newcastle-upon-Tyne, to make a Branch Railway, and for other purposes connected with their undertaking'.
>
> And it is intended by the said Act, so to be applied for, to take Powers to alter and vary the Branch Railway, extending from the Newcastle-upon-Tyne and Carlisle Railway, at or near Haltwhistle, to Alston and Nenthead, authorised to be made by the said Act, by abandoning so much of the said Branch Railway as extends between the point of junction with the Newcastle-upon-Tyne and Carlisle Railway in the Township of Haltwhistle, in the Parish of Haltwhistle in the County of Northumberland . . . and . . . a field called Broomhouse Meadow, belonging to Cuthbert Ellison, Esquire, and occupied by John Waugh, situate in the Township of Bellister in the Parish of Haltwhistle.

In place of this railway, the Newcastle & Carlisle company proposed to make a new connection with the main line which would pass through the 'Parishes, Townships, Townlands and extra-parochial places' of 'Haltwhistle, Plenmeller and Bellister' and terminate 'in the said field called Broomhouse Meadow'. At Alston, the company sought consent to abandon:

> So much of the said branch railway . . . as extends between a Point or Place . . . in a field belonging to the Commissioners and Governors of Greenwich Hospital, occupied by Rebecca Walton, situate in the Township and Parish of Alston Moor, otherwise Alston, otherwise Aldstone, in the County of Cumberland, and the western terminus of the said branch railway in the Chapelry of Nent Head, in the said Parish of Alston Moor.

Elsewhere, the company intended to make various alterations to the authorised route between Haltwhistle and Alston; in the parish of Lambley, for example, the amended line was to run further east than had originally been intended, while further alterations would result in the deviation of much of the earlier route. At the same time, the new scheme featured an entirely new branch, which was intended to provide a useful connection between the Alston line and the nearby Brampton Railway. This new branch was defined as:

> A Branch Railway, with all necessary and convenient works connected therewith, to commence at or upon the . . . line of railway . . . in a plantation belonging to and in the occupation of Thomas Whitfield, situate in the said Township of Lambley, otherwise Lamley . . . and . . . terminate at or upon a Part or Point . . . of a Railway belonging to the Earl of Carlisle, situate at Haltonian Gate, in the Township of Hartley Burn, in the said Parish of Haltwhistle.

It was hoped that the amended Alston scheme could be accomplished 'partly from the Sum of Two hundred and forty thousand Pounds', authorised to be raised by the original 1846 Newcastle & Carlisle Act, and 'partly from the Sum of Eighty thousand Pounds authorised to be borrowed by the said Company' under that same Act; in fact, the new scheme would enable many small savings to be made because the works proposed by the amended Bill were 'less in magnitude and estimated expense' than those envisaged in 1846.

The new Bill was placed before Parliament in the early months of 1849, and on 13th July, 1849 the revised Alston branch proposals received the Royal Assent. The new Act (12 & 13 Vic. cap. 43) provided consent for a 13 mile branch from Haltwhistle to Alston, together with a short spur running westwards from Lambley to an end-on junction with the Earl of Carlisle's Brampton Railway.

The amended route followed the South Tyne Valley, keeping close to the river and climbing steadily from an elevation of 405 ft above mean sea level at Haltwhistle to a summit of over 900 ft at Alston; gradients would average about 1 in 100/1 in 150, but the steepest sections included a formidable stretch of 1 in 56 between Slaggyford and Alston. The chosen route entailed considerable engineering work, and there would be major river crossings at Haltwhistle and Lambley, together with numerous smaller bridges and culverts.

Construction Begins

The route was staked out at the end of 1849, and the major construction contracts were let in the following year. Work was under way by the early months of 1850, and at the half-year meeting held in Newcastle-upon-Tyne on 28th March the assembled Newcastle & Carlisle shareholders learned that their Directors were at last paying 'very serious attention to the Alston branch'. Construction was in progress, and negotiations had been opened with 'the proprietors of the land required'. A few months later, it was announced that an outlay of £20,000 would be needed 'to finish the Alston branch'.

Work proceeded throughout the rest of 1850 and 1851, and having made considerable progress at the northern end, the Directors decided that goods traffic could be introduced between Haltwhistle and Shaft Hill, a distance of 4¼ miles. The first trains apparently ran in March 1851, and on 5th April *The Railway Times* reported that the branch was 'progressing', a portion from Haltwhistle to near Lambley being 'already in use for the conveyance of minerals and goods'.

Similar progress had been made at the southern end of the line, and although there was no immediate prospect of running from Alston to the temporary railhead at Shaft Hill, the presence of a branch of the Brampton Railway at Midgeholme suggested that an alternative route might be created for goods traffic between Alston, Lambley, and the Newcastle & Carlisle main line at Brampton Junction. Accordingly, in January 1852, mineral trains commenced running to Alston via the Brampton Railway. In March 1852 the Newcastle & Carlisle Directors reported that the line was 'open at both ends' and would be opened throughout 'on the completion of the viaduct over the Vale of the South Tyne at Lambley'. This impressive structure had nine 58 ft-span arches and seven 20 ft spans; its height above water level was about 100 ft, and the viaduct was approached by sharp curves on either side.

The Alston branch was finally opened throughout on 17th November, 1852, but in common with many other lines, it seems that the route had been rushed into use before it was properly completed, and it is likely that local travellers were subjected to considerable inconvenience during the initial months of operation. Stations, for example, were probably still being painted and decorated, while ancillary items such as telegraph poles were not yet in place.

Four months later, in March 1853, the Newcastle & Carlisle shareholders were informed that the branch was 'so far finished that it would come under the same arrangements as the main line from 1st April', but adverse weather conditions had impeded the installation of telegraph equipment and the necessary posts were not yet erected. On 1st April, however, the telegraph would be brought into use*, and it was also announced that five stations on the branch and on the main line would be 'worked by clerks'. (The stations involved were presumably Haltwhistle, Featherstone, Lambley, Slaggyford and Alston itself.)

The completed branch was soon carrying significant quantities of goods and mineral traffic, and there seemed every reason to agree with the Directors' claim that the Alston branch would be 'greatly favourable to the parent line'. It would, they hoped, 'greatly increase the traffic and have a salutary effect upon their dividends . . . a great deal of traffic would be brought upon the line'. There was also talk of the distance from Alston to

* According to the NER Appendix to Working Timetable for 1874, only Alston had a telegraph instrument at that date.

Newcastle being just fifty two miles - the implications of this statement being that some through running may have been contemplated. In the event, passenger trains generally terminated at Haltwhistle, and timetables suggest that through running never became an established feature of Alston branch operation; in any case, the altered junction arrangements at Haltwhistle did not permit through running towards Newcastle, and the little through working that did, in fact, take place was generally to and from Carlisle.

Some Details of the Line

The new railway was heavily engineered, and beside the many-spanned South Tyne Viaduct at Lambley and an equally-impressive 6-arched viaduct at Haltwhistle, the route incorporated eight smaller viaducts with spans ranging from 20 ft to 30 ft (see *Table 5*). Bridges and other works were, in most cases, wide enough to accommodate a second line of rails if growing traffic should ever justify such a facility, and most structures were solidly built of local stone. There were, in all, no less than 60* bridges, viaducts and culverts on the 13-mile single track route between Haltwhistle and Alston.

At Alston, the branch ended in an attractive Elizabethan-style terminus with a miniature overall roof, while the intermediate stopping places at Featherstone, Lambley and Slaggyford were each provided with substantial two-storey station houses for the 'station clerks' (i.e. station masters) and their families.

Alston station occupied a picturesque (though slightly cramped) riverside position near the confluence of the rivers Nent and South Tyne, but there was nevertheless sufficient room for a fairly capacious goods yard between the passenger station and the Hexham Road. A large goods shed was provided in the yard at Alston, though Lambley and the other wayside stations were equipped only with loading docks and small goods lock-ups; NER-type coal drops were provided at each station.

Early train services were modest in the extreme. In 1858, for example, the first up passenger train left Alston at 7.28 am and arrived in Haltwhistle by 8.16 am. A balancing down working left the junction at 8.38 am and arrived back in Alston at 9.26. There was, thereafter, an enormous gap (in which the branch engine presumably undertook goods duties) and the next up service did not leave Alston until 5.28 pm. This working reached Haltwhistle at 6.16 pm and returned to Alston at 7 pm. Study of these timings indicates that the branch engine was stationed at Alston, an engine shed and turntable being provided at the end of the line. Another turntable was available at Haltwhistle, suggesting that the Alston route was worked sometimes by former main line tender locomotives that were turned at the end of each short journey.

Effects of the Railway

The opening of the railway dealt an immediate body-blow to the horse-drawn passenger services that had hitherto provided a somewhat tenuous

* An additional bridge was built at Alston around 1908 when one of the goods sidings was extended beneath the Hexham Road to reach a stone yard; this extra bridge became No. 61 in the Alston branch bridge numbering system.

link between Penrith, Alston and the N&C main line at Hexham. More importantly, the new branch line was of great benefit to the mining industry, and in his book *Iron Ores of Great Britain* (1856) W.W. Smyth related how the opening of the branch enabled new mineral veins to be profitably exploited:

> The majority of the mineral veins or lodes of the Alston district, celebrated for their productiveness of lead ore, range nearly from east to west . . . Some of these lead veins, in part of their course, are charged with brown iron ore instead of the usual veinstone of flour spar and quartz and its concomitant lead ore. Thus the rich lode of Rodderup Fell where it crosses the valley of the Tyne, above Alston and is known as the Craig Green or Bracken Syke vein, is seen in the so-called 'scar' limestone, as a vein of brown ore from 16 to 20 feet in width. Hitherto, however, from the remote position of the district, these repositories of an ore so well calculated to produce a good quality of iron have been very little explored.
>
> Since the late extension of a branch railway to the town of Alston certain of the lodes, apparently producing nothing but this kind of ore, have been extensively wrought. Thus the Manor House vein has been opened up very near the railway station for the Shotley Bridge Company, and hundreds of tons have been raised from a very small area at the extremely low cost of 1*s.* 7*d.* per ton . . . on the opposite side of the valley of the Tyne, the Park or Horse Edge vein has also lately been wrought, and considerable quantities of a similar brown ore are now being raised from the Thorngill vein where it intersects the 'great' limestone.

Unfortunately, the opening of the railway coincided with the onset of a depression in the lead industry, and although, for a few years, the Alston mines produced around 5,000 tons of lead ore, decline became more pronounced by about 1870. The decline of the lead industry was reflected in a falling population, and whereas the Alston area was inhabited by 6,815 people in 1851, there were only 5,680 inhabitants in Alston, Nenthead and Garrigill in 1871, and just 4,621 by 1881.

The steady decrease in lead production and corresponding decrease in local population meant that the line was not as profitable as it would otherwise have been, but the railway was nevertheless of vital importance to South Tynedale in that it enabled local mining companies to exploit, not just lead, but various other minerals. Zinc, for instance, was destined to become of increasing importance in the later 19th century — the reason being that zinc or 'spelter' was needed for galvanised iron production and also for use in the infant electrical industry.

Of equal (if not greater) importance in terms of freight traffic, was the development of coal mining in the South Tyne Valley. Although there had been many small coal mines in the area in pre-railway days, the opening of the line provided even greater scope for the development of coal mining operations. As we shall see, the railway eventually served at least four relatively large pits by direct rail sidings, and other mines were linked to the branch by a series of connecting tramways. Quarrying, too, developed as a larger-scale industry after the opening of the line, and taking all of these factors into consideration, it is clear that — despite the decline of the lead industry after 1870 — the Alston branch fulfilled its primary function as a vital transport link between an important mining and quarrying area and the outside world.

In a footnote, it is interesting to find that the original Alston branch buildings were said to have been designed by the Newcastle architects John and Benjamin Green, who also carried out much work on the neighbouring North Eastern Railway and its constituents. Perhaps for this reason, there were marked similarities between the Alston branch stations and NER stations such as Beal and Tynemouth (old) station, both of which featured the Jacobean gables and details seen at Alston, Lambley and Slaggyford. The Greens were a father and son partnership, Benjamin (the son) being a noted architect with many fine buildings to his credit — among them the Theatre Royal in Newcastle-upon-Tyne.

A busy scene at Alston station around 1920. The branch passenger train stands beneath the overall roof station while the tender locomotive shunts the yard.

Lens of Sutton

The working timetable for the Branch dated 1st April, 1870.

ALSTON BRANCH.—The trains on the Alston Branch must be worked strictly in accordance with the Train Staff Regulations.

Alston Branch. / **SUN.**

		1	2	3	4	5	SUN. 1	SUN. 2
Down.	Distance.	Pass.	Pass.	Goods.	Mineral.	Pass.		
	Mls.	a.m.	p.m.	p.m.	p.m.	p.m.		
HALTWHISTLE	...	8 59	12 2	3 0	3 15	7 8	...	...
Featherstone ...	3	9 9	12 12	3 15	...	7 18	...	...
Shaft Hill	4	9 13	12 16	3 20	3 35	7 22	...	...
Lambley	4½	9 16	12 19	3 50	...	7 25	...	...
Slaggyford	8½	9 27	12 30	4 10	...	7 36	...	...
ALSTON	13	9 39	12 42	4 30	...	7 48		...
Up.	Mls.	a.m.	a.m.	p.m.		p.m.		
ALSTON	..	7 25	10 41	1 15	...	5 25	...	...
Slaggyford	4¾	7 37	10 53	1 35	...	5 37	...	...
Lambley	8½	7 48	11 4	1 50		5 48	...	...
Shaft Hill	9	7 51	11 7	1 55	4 0	5 51	...	...
Featherstone	10	7 55	11 11	2 0	...	5 55	...	...
HALTWHISTLE	13	8 5	11 21	2 15	4 20	6 5	...	...

Staff Stations—Haltwhistle Junction, Shaft Hill, and Alston.

Chapter Two

A North Eastern Branch Line (1862–1948)

The Newcastle & Carlisle Railway was, at one time, at the centre of much bickering between rival railway companies; the London & North Western and North British companies were both keen to assume control of the route — both protagonists being aware that possession of the Newcastle company would give them direct access to Tyneside. Ironically, the LNWR and NBR failed in their attempt to gain control of the Newcastle & Carlisle line, and on 17th July, 1862 the Newcastle company passed into the open hands of the North Eastern Railway. Itself an amalgam of the Leeds Northern, York & North Midland, and York, Newcastle & Berwick railways, the North Eastern Railway had been formed in 1854; a further amalgamation, in 1863, added the pioneering Stockton & Darlington Railway to the burgeoning NER system.

As a result of these successive amalgamations, the North Eastern Railway became an immensely-successful mineral-carrying railway, with a firm power base in the industrial areas of Northumberland and Durham. The Alston branch was, in many ways, an ideal addition to the growing NER system, and in subsequent years the Haltwhistle to Alston route was progressively transformed into a typical North Eastern Railway branch line.

Improving the Branch

The North Eastern initiated many small improvements at Alston and elsewhere. In February 1866, for instance, the NER agreed that the sum of £33 could be expended in order to provide 'a small office . . . in the goods warehouse at Alston', and in May 1868 the Way & Works Committee decided that extra accommodation 'for the loading of cattle and sheep' would be provided at Alston 'as recommended by the Traffic Committee at a cost not exceeding £20'. At Haltwhistle, meanwhile, the company had ordered a new turntable in February 1865 because the original one was 'insufficient for the requirements of that station'.

Further improvements were made at Alston during the early 1870s when the NER carried out an extensive rebuilding programme. It was agreed that the existing train shed was too small and (perhaps more importantly) too low, and on 15th May, 1872 the company accepted a tender of £446 13*s*. 4*d*. for reconstruction of the shed roof. As a result of these improvements the original arc-roofed shed was taken down, and in its place Alston station gained a distinctive double-pitched gambrel roof.

When first opened the intermediate stations at Featherstone, Lambley and Slaggyford had featured solidly-built station houses, but passenger facilities were extremely primitive, and to rectify this situation it appears that the NER added timber-built waiting rooms to the original stone buildings. As a corollary of these improvements the company also raised the station platforms to a height commensurate with modern traffic requirements, while in 1878–79* the NER spent £672 on an entirely new station at Shaft Hill on the site of the temporary stopping place used from 1851 until 1852. The new station was a cheaply-built, timber structure, but this utilitarian stopping

* The contract drawings for the stone station master's house was signed by the NER Architect, Wm. Peachey (23rd October, 1876) and by his successor Wm. Bell (20th October, 1876).

place was welcomed by local cottagers who no longer had to cross the intervening river in order to reach Lambley station!

Locomotives and Train Services in the NER Era

The original train service of two up and two down workings had increased to three trains each way by the 1870s. In November 1873, for instance, the branch carried three up and three down trains between Alston and Haltwhistle, but there were no Sunday services. This basic pattern of services had increased to four trains in each direction by the turn-of-the-century, and in June 1912 trains left Alston for Haltwhistle at 7.10, 10 am, 2.15 and 6.30 pm, returning from the junction at 8.20, 11.50 am, 4.15 and 7.33 pm, respectively. An additional evening train ran on Saturdays, and the Sunday service provided two up and two down workings.

This timetable persisted, with very little alteration, until the end of the NER period, and in April 1920 there were still only four trains each way; up workings left Alston at 7.05, 10 am, 1.55 and 6.55 pm, while balancing down services departed from Haltwhistle at 8.05, 11.45 am, 4.20 and 8 pm. On Saturdays the last down working left Haltwhistle at the later time of 8.15 pm, and arrived at Alston by 8.50 pm. The usual journey time was 35 minutes, although some trains were allowed slightly longer journey times for the 13 mile journey — this allowed time for an additional stop at an unadvertised halt serving Plenmeller Colliery (between Haltwhistle and Featherstone). The halt had been opened in 1919, and although it did not appear in public timetables the new stopping place resulted in a considerable amount of extra workmens' traffic between Alston and Haltwhistle.

Alston Branch

Down.	Distance.	1 Pass.	2 Goods.	3 Pass.	4 Mineral.	5 PASS. Saturdays only.	6 Pass.		SUN.	
	Mls.	a.m.	a.m.	a.m	p.m.	• p m	p.m.			
HALTWHISTLE ....Dep.	...	8 30	10 55	11 36	3 15	4 15	7 40	...	..	..
Featherstone .... "	3	8 39	..	11 44	...	4 24	7 49	...	..	..
Shaft Hill .... "	4	8 43	..	11 48	3 35	4 28	7 53	...	..	..
Lambley........................ "	4½	8 46	12 5	11 51	...	4 31	7 56	...	..	..
Slaggyford .... "	8¾	8 55	..	12 0	...	4 40	8 5	...	..	..
ALSTON ... .Arr.		9 5	12 30	12 10		4 50	8 15	..	..	..

Staff Stations.—Haltwhistle Junction, Shaft Hill, and Alston. The following are the sections into which this branch is divided as described in paragraph 2 of *Regulations* for working single lines, see pages of appendix: Haltwhistle Junction and Shaft Hill; Shaft Hill and Alston.

omn... carriage is attached to this train for the conveyance of passengers. ... must be particul...

Up.	Distance	1 Pass.	2 Pass.	3 Goods.	4 PASS. Saturday only.	5 Mineral.	6 Pass.		SUN.	
	Mls.	a.m.	a.m.	B p.m.	p m		p.m.			
ALSTON ....Dep.		7 20	10 5	1 0	2 25	..	5 40	...	..	..
Slaggyford .... "	4¼	7 30	10 15	1 15	2 35	...	5 50	...	..	..
Lambley .... "	8½	7 39	10 24	1 30	2 44		5 59	...	..	..
Shaft Hill..................... "	9	7 42	10 27	1 40	2 47	4 0	6 2	...	..	..
Featherstone .... "	10	7 46	10 31	1 50	2 51	..	6 6	...	..	..
HALTWHISTLE ....Arr.	13	7 55	10 40	2 0	3 0	4 20	6 15	...	..	..

...ar in stopping carriage at station platforms.

Working timetable for May 1884 for the Branch.

Indeed, for a few years the colliery worked day and night, and it was usual, around 1920, for the branch train service to commence at the early hour of 2.10 am to cater for shift workers travelling to and from the pit.

Public timetables gave no indication of the extent of night-time activity on the Alston branch, but the late Ken Hoole very kindly noted down the following summary of branch engine working for the Winter of 1922, and study of these engine timings will reveal the full extent of miners' traffic at the end of the NER period.

Engine Working — Winter 1922 (Weekdays)

	arrive	*depart*	*Notes*
	am	am	
Alston	–	3.00	Workmens' train (SX)
Haltwhistle	3.45	3.58	Workmens' train (MSX*)
Alston	4.39	–	
Alston	–	7.05	Public working
Haltwhistle	7.40	8.05	Public working
Alston	8.40	10.00	Public working
Haltwhistle	10.35	11.50	Public working (calls Plenmeller)
	pm	pm	
Alston	12.25	–	
Alston	–	1.55	Public working
Haltwhistle	2.30	4.20	Public working
Alston	4.55	6.55	Public working (calls Plenmeller)
Haltwhistle	7.30	8.00	Public working (SX)
Alston	8.35	–	
Haltwhistle	–	8.15	Public working (SO)
Alston	8.50	–	

* Ran empty MO, arriving Alston at 4.28 am

The above timings relate only to passenger working, the usual practice, around 1920–1939, being for Carlisle-based locomotives to work the branch goods and mineral trains. Nevertheless, the branch passenger service was intensive enough to require three separate train crews, and in October 1922 the three crews changed shifts at the following times:

1st Set		*2nd Set*		*3rd Set*	
Alston	2.05 am	Alston	9.45 am	Alston	1.45 pm
Alston	10.05 am	Alston	5.45 pm	Alston	9.45 pm

As mentioned earlier the Alston route was probably worked by former main line engines during the middle years of the 19th century, but standard North Eastern branch line classes appeared in increasing numbers towards the end of the Victorian period, and by 1900 the famous Bogie Tank Passenger ('BTP') 0–4–4Ts had become the usual Alston branch engines. Designed by E. Fletcher, the 'BTP' class was introduced in 1874, and 124 of these local passenger engines were eventually built. Engines known to have worked on the Alston branch include No. 319 and the unfortunate No. 69

which, in 1920, ran away from Alston engine shed and ended up on its side in the river; the engine was soon recovered, but for many years thereafter coupling chains, a buffer and other relics of the accident could be glimpsed at the bottom of the 'station pool'.

Another class seen on the Alston to Haltwhistle line in the North Eastern period was T.W. Worsdell's 'class A' 2–4–2 passenger tanks. Introduced in 1886, the 'class As' were remarkably similar to the 'M15' 2–4–2Ts designed by Worsdell for the Great Eastern Railway. Their 5 ft 7¼ in. coupled wheels were, perhaps, better-suited to fast suburban work than toiling up and down the steeply-graded Alston branch, but the 'class As' were nevertheless used sporadically on the branch during the early 1900s.

In earlier years, a single locomotive had been out-stationed at Alston for both passenger *and* freight work, but at the turn-of-the-century the usual allocation was two engines — an 0–4–4T or 2–4–2T passenger locomotive, and an 0–6–0 for goods work. There was, however, no hard and fast rule about the use of Alston-based engines for both passenger and goods work, and as we have seen, Carlisle engines worked branch goods services at the end of the NER period (and during the LNER era prior to World War II).

Passenger vehicles used on the Alston to Haltwhistle line during the later NER period were usually 52 ft eliptical roof bogie coaches, the normal branch set being brake composite No. 3688 and sister vehicle No. 3692. Both vehicles had been built at York in 1907 to carriage diagrams Nos. 124 and 125. They were lit by electricity, and ran in a set formation with a guard's compartment at each end. As a general rule, these two coaches did not leave the branch unless they had to undergo major maintenance operations; routine cleaning was carried out under the station roof at Alston, a vacuum cleaner van being sent out to the terminus for this purpose. The latter vehicle was a former 6-wheeled NER brake third, which was allocated to the Newcastle district and covered several local branch lines (among them the Allendale, Rothbury and Reedsmouth lines).

Although the Alston branch train was a set rake of two brake composites, it was necessary for spare vehicles to be stationed at Alston for strengthening purposes, and for this reason a third class coach was usually parked on the carriage siding beneath the station roof. The 'spare' vehicle was changed at regular intervals and it is impossible to say, with any degree of precision, which coaches were used for strengthening purposes during the NER era.

Passenger and Goods Traffic

The Alston branch served a lightly-populated rural area, and passenger traffic was not particularly heavy. In 1901, for example, Alston station issued only 14,540 tickets, while in 1911, this meagre figure had decreased to just 12,349 — representing an average of around 13,350 passenger bookings a year. To put these figures into perspective it would be useful to compare Alston's passenger bookings with those from comparable branch line stations in other parts of the country, and *Table 2* makes such a comparison between Alston and three similar branch line termini. It will be seen that Alston's annual passenger bookings were less than those from Tetbury and Woodstock, but the North Eastern terminus issued considerably more tickets than Fairford. These figures would suggest that, if Alston was hardly a busy station, it was by no means under-utilised in comparison with certain other rural stations.

Table 2

COMPARATIVE PASSENGER BOOKINGS FOR ALSTON AND OTHER STATIONS

Station	*Year*	*Tickets Issued*
Tetbury (GWR)	1903	17,664
Tetbury (GWR)	1913	17,809
Blenheim & Woodstock (GWR)	1903	17,436
Blenheim & Woodstock (GWR)	1913	17,168
Alston (NER)	1901	14,540
Alston (NER)	1911	12,349
Fairford (GWR)	1903	7,672
Fairford (GWR)	1913	6,882

Freight traffic was an important element in branch operation, and although small stations such as Lambley or Slaggyford did not in themselves contribute much traffic, the presence of private sidings at various places *en route* to Alston ensured that the line carried large quantities of coal and stone. These were, at one time, several of these private sidings between Haltwhistle and Alston, and in addition to the colliery sidings at Lambley and Plenmeller, there were further mine or quarry sidings at Featherstone, Slaggyford, Coanwood and Alston stations. These sidings were at their peak during the early 1900s, but thereafter the number of rail-served mines and

A distant view of Slaggyford station, probably photographed in the 1920s. The wooden booking office and waiting room can be seen to the left, while the large N&CR station master's house is visible behind the signal box. *Courtesy Ruby Makepeace*

quarries decreased as the mines concerned became exhausted or uneconomic to work.

Alston and the intermediate stations were equipped with coal staithes, loading docks and cattle pens, and the following table (compiled with the aid of successive editions of the *Railway Clearing House Handbook of Stations*) will give some idea of the kind of goods facilities available on the Alston branch. For convenience, all private sidings are shown, though it should be stressed that not all of these sidings were in use at the same time (*see Chapter Three for further details*).

Table 3

STATION ACCOMMODATION AND PRIVATE SIDINGS c.1900–1923

Station	*m.*	*ch.*	*Facilities*	*Crane*	*Private sidings*
Haltwhistle	00	00	G P F L H C	3 ton	Various private sidings
Plenmeller	00	79	P	–	Plenmeller Colliery
Featherstone	03	07	G P F L H C	2 ton	Featherstone Colliery
Coanwood	04	18	G P L H	1 ton	Coanwood Colliery Coanwood Whinstone Quarry
Lambley	04	67	G P L H	–	Lambley Colliery Midgeholme Colliery
Slaggyford	08	49	G P L H	–	Anthracite Coal & Lime Co. Barhaugh Anthracite & Lime Co.
Alston	13	14	G P F L H C	3 ton	Alston Lime Siding Alston & Nentforce Quarry Co. Vielle Montague Zinc Co.

Key G = Goods; P = Passengers; F = Loading dock for furniture, machinery, motor vehicles, etc.; L = Cattle and Livestock; H = Horses; C = Cars and carriages

Study of this table will reveal that Coanwood, Lambley and Slaggyford were not equipped with end-loading docks for furniture or vehicle traffic, whereas Haltwhistle, Alston and Featherstone were fully equipped with a wide range of facilities for all forms of traffic. These arrangements remained unchanged for many years, but Featherstone Park was later down-graded when, in a search for economies, the LNER withdrew cattle-handling facilities. The station also lost its crane, although, if necessary, rail-mounted cranes could be sent to handle occasional heavy consignments.

The volume of goods and minerals handled at each station varied from year to year, but generally speaking Alston handled up to 9,000 tons of ore per annum during the early 1900s, while in a good year Lambley dealt with around 50,000 tons of minerals. In 1895, for example, Lambley handled 48,566 tons of coal, limestone and related traffic. However, these figures fluctuated in relation to the changing fortunes and transient nature of the mining industry, and by 1923 Alston's annual ore traffic had declined to just 2,000 tons; stone traffic, in contrast, had risen to some 25,000 tons a year, and this welcome increase more than compensated for the reduction in ore traffic.

Livestock constituted a small, but relatively stable source of revenue at Alston and the intermediate stations. In general, Alston dealt with 200–300 wagonloads of cattle or sheep a year during the later NER period, while Slaggyford handled about 100 wagonloads a year during the same period. The other stations handled rather less livestock — probably because local farmers could easily receive or despatch cattle from neighbouring Haltwhistle; in 1908 Featherstone Park dealt with 48 wagonloads, the corresponding figures for Lambley and Coanwood being 22 and 6 respectively.

There was a daily pick-up goods train from Carlisle to Alston, and at the turn-of-the-century this daily working reached the terminus at a little after noon, having called at all of the intermediate stations; there was also (1904) a separate train worked through from Blaydon, while other trains were run to serve the colliery sidings at Featherstone, Coanwood and Lambley. Cattle traffic was important enough to justify the provision of special trains on market days, and such workings usually ran through from Alston to Carlisle (or vice versa).

Freight vehicles seen on the Alston branch were predominantly open wagons, and old photographs show that the NER's characteristic wooden hopper wagons were widely-used (these vehicles had clearly been developed from the primitive wooden tub wagons used in northern collieries since the early days of the Industrial Revolution). General merchandise was transported in 5-plank opens or covered vans, while timber or other specialised types of freight traffic was brought into the area on bolster wagons, flat trucks or on special machinery-carrying vehicles. Cattle were conveyed in cattle wagons, most of which would probably have been NER vehicles — although rolling stock from the North British Railway or other neighbouring companies would have appeared from time to time.

The Grouping and After

In 1923 the independent life of the North Eastern Railway came to an end, for the Government had decided (as an alternative to nationalisation in the changing economic climate after World War I) that the main line railway companies would be grouped into four large regional organisations. The necessary Act of Parliament was obtained in 1921, and on 1st January, 1923 the NER was merged with the Great Northern, Great Central, Great Eastern, North British, Great North of Scotland (and other companies) to form the aptly-named London & North Eastern Railway. The new company was an extensive and somewhat ramshackle undertaking, and the LNER management was faced with an immense task as it sought ways of unifying its hitherto-disparate constituents.

In the short term, the 1923 grouping produced few obvious changes, and most ordinary travellers would have been unaware that a momentous change of ownership had in fact taken place. In the ensuing months, however, the LNER introduced its own liveries, and as a result the regular Alston branch passenger train was repainted in a sombre brown colour scheme in place of the plum red livery that had been carried during the NER era. The two branch coaches were also renumbered, No. 3688 becoming No. 23688, while its running mate became No. 23692. Fitted freight stock, meanwhile, received a new reddish brown livery in place of the NER's grey colour scheme, while the attractive North Eastern locomotive livery was replaced by utilitarian black — only engines with wheels larger than 6 ft 6 in. being considered important enough to carry LNER apple green livery.

Apart from these new liveries, the LNER initiated an entirely new system of locomotive class notation based upon engine wheelbases. The new system was both logical and simple in that 4–6–2s became 'As', 4–6–0s became 'Bs', 4–4–2s became 'Cs', 4–4–0s became 'Ds' and so on. As there was usually more than one type of engine with a particular wheelbase these basic notations were further sub-divided by the addition of a numerical suffix — thus the familiar Bogie Tank Passenger 0–4–4Ts became LNER class 'G6', while the former North Eastern class 'A' 2–4–2Ts became LNER class 'F8'. Both of these classes remained at work on the Alston line during the immediate post-grouping period, typical numbers, around 1924, being 'F8' 2–4–2Ts Nos. 1599 and 172.

Other types of locomotive used on the branch during the post-1923 period included 'N8' 0–6–2Ts, 'J21' 0–6–0s and 'G5' 0–4–4Ts. From 1930 until 1933, for instance, the regular branch engine was 'N8' 0–6–2T No. 863, while from 1936 until 1940 the usual Alston locomotive was 'J21' No. 51. Introduced in 1886, the 'N8' class was a mixed traffic design, intended for use on local passenger and freight duties; designed by T.W. Worsdell, they had 19 in. × 24 in. cylinders and 5 ft 1¼ in. coupled wheels (some later received 19 in. × 26 in. cylinders). They were, in many ways, ideally-suited for use on the heavily-graded Alston branch, and it is perhaps surprising that they were not used throughout the LNER era. In retrospect, the ex-NER locomotives most readily-associated with the Alston line were the 'G5' 0–4–4Ts; several of these engines worked on the route at various times, among them Nos. 1788 and 1838 — both of which appeared during the 1930s.

The 'G5s' were unsuitable for hauling goods traffic on the Alston branch, but as freight duties were undertaken by 'J21s', 'J25s' or other 0–6–0 types, this deficiency was of little consequence. (In the 1930s, Alston freight services were still worked by Carlisle-based locomotives, and these engines also worked some of the branch passenger turns.) An unusual visitor, around 1937, was 'A8' 4–6–2T No. 2146, which was noted at the head of a four-coach passenger train composed of three eliptical-roof coaches and one clerestory roof vehicle; the 'A8' class had been rebuilt from former NER class 'D' 4–4–4Ts (LNER class 'H1') between 1931 and 1936.

The 1930s were a period of change in which the LNER introduced several small innovations in an attempt to reduce expenditure and increase efficiency. In 1933, for example, the Alston to Lambley single line section was converted from staff-and-ticket to electric token operation, and at the same time a motorised platelayers' trolley was introduced so that permanent way men no longer had to patrol the line on foot.* In the event, this vehicle was used for only five years, and after 1938 daily track inspection was again carried out on foot (it is assumed that the rising gradients between Halt-

* This now meant that the trackwalker would now travel considerably further than his two to three miles of his original 'length'.

whistle and Alston mitigated against the use of a motorised trolley).

Meanwhile, industrial change had resulted in the abandonment of several mines and quarries. Plenmeller Colliery, for instance, was closed in 1932, while neighbouring Coanwood Colliery had been closed in 1917 (although small-scale mining operations continued in the immediate vicinity). There was similar industrial retraction at Slaggyford, where the Barhaugh Anthracite & Limestone Company was closed around 1938.

The following table underlines the essentially temporary nature of mines and quarries which flourished briefly for a few years and then vanished once seams became exhausted or too difficult to work. The name of each mine is followed by the name of each mining company — though it should be stressed that mines could (and did) change ownership, and some mines were worked by different mining companies at different times. The next five columns relate to the combined underground and surface labour forces needed to work each pit, and finally, the extreme right hand column lists some general data about each pit; the numbers of people employed will of course give an approximate indication of the relative size of each colliery — and it will be seen that some of the local mines were very small scale operations that would have yielded little traffic for the railway.

Trains and Traffic in the LNER Period

There were, for many years, just four trains each way between Alston and Haltwhistle. In September 1925, for example, trains left Alston at 7.05, 10.00 am, 1.55 and 6.55 pm; the balancing down workings left Haltwhistle at 8.05, 11.47 am, 4.18 and 8 pm, but there was, by that time, no longer a Sunday service.

In addition to the regular branch passenger services, there were also several unadvertised workmens' trains between Alston and Haltwhistle — some of which called at Plenmeller Colliery Halt between Haltwhistle and Featherstone Park. Sadly, this unadvertised halt was closed in the early 1930s following the demise of Plenmeller Colliery.

The Winter 1933 public timetable was similar to its 1925 predecessor, and there were again four trains in each direction, the times of departure from Alston being 7.05, 10.10 am, 1.41 and 6.50 pm, while return workings left Haltwhistle at 8.05, 11.50 am, 4.36 and 8 pm. Saturdays-only services left Alston at 5.20 and 9.10 pm, with return trips from the junction at 6.10 and 10.37 pm; an additional down service departed from Haltwhistle (SO) at 8.15 pm.

The timetable in operation on the eve of World War II was relatively complex by Alston branch standards, with six advertised trains each way daily. In the up direction, there were departures from Alston at 7.10, 10.15 am, 12.35, 3.55, 7 and 8.20 pm, with corresponding return trips from Haltwhistle at 8.10, 11.30 am, 1.35, 5.05, 6.20 and 9.10 pm. The 8.20 pm from Alston was a through working to Carlisle, but curiously, public timetables did not show any down workings *from* Carlisle, to Alston. Such workings were in fact provided — although they fulfilled no real public need and were a result of overall timetable planning rather than an overt desire to improve local train services.

Table 4

MINING ACTIVITIES IN THE ALSTON AREA 1910–1941

Name(s)	*Owners*	*1899*	*1910*	*1925*	*1930*	*1941*	*Notes*
Plenmeller	Plenmeller Collieries Ltd	88	3	372	337	–	Closed 1932
Featherstone No. 6 Pit	Featherstone Colliery Co.	–	–	–	–	3	Closed June 1941
Featherstone	Thompson & Sons, Brampton Jn	228	–	–	–	–	Closed 1905
Coanwood* (Herdley Bank Pit)	Coanwood Coal Co.	23	49	–	–	–	Closed 1917
Herdman's Drift* (Coanwood)	Herdman & Co.	–	–	–	3	–	
East Coanwood*		–	–	–	–	–	Closed pre-1900
Slaggyford (Barhaugh)	Barhaugh Anthracite & Lime Co.	–	3	14	5	–	Closed c.1938
Slaggyford (Snope Burn)	Snope Burn Anthracite Coal Co.	–	3	–	–	–	'Temporarily closed' 1927, and abandoned 1940
Ayle (Alston)	Ayle Colliery Ltd	–	–	–	–	0	Abandoned June 1941
Alston Drift	W. Benson & Son	17	–	–	–	–	
Lambley	Lambley Coal Co.	–	26	60	75	80	
Newshield Quarry (Coatleyhill, Alston)	Alston Lime & Coal Co.	17	n/a	n/a	n/a	n/a	
Rock House Drift* (Coanwood)	G.J. & H.C. Ridley	–	–	–	–	5	
Crystal Well* (Coanwood)	J. Ridley	–	–	–	–	8	
Whalley Drift* (Coanwood)		–	–	–	–	–	Abandoned 1904
Nenthead	Vielle Montagne Zinc Co.	418	n/a	n/a	n/a	n/a	
Coanwood Whinstone Quarry	Coanwood Whinstone Co.	46	n/a	–	–	–	

NB. Mines marked * occupied a small geographical area and invariably tapped the same seam. It follows that there may be confusion between the various Coanwood pits, some of which were 'closed' mines re-entered by local miners.

The apparent simplicity of the branch passenger timetable masked some surprisingly complex engine workings involving locomotives from both Alston and Carlisle sheds. The late Ken Hoole very generously provided the following summary of branch engine working for May 1939, and these timings form a useful supplement to the 1939 passenger timetable.

Engine Working — May 1939 (Weekdays)

	arrive	*depart*	*Notes*
	am	am	
Shed	–	6.55	Light engine
Alston	–	7.10	Passenger
Haltwhistle	7.41	8.10	Passenger
Alston	8.42	10.15	Passenger
Haltwhistle	10.41	11.35	Passenger (then shunts yard)
	pm	pm	
Alston	12.07	–	Light engine (to shed)
Shed	12.10	3.40	Light engine
Alston	–	3.55	Passenger
Haltwhistle	4.26	5.05	Passenger
Alston	5.37	7.00	Passenger
Haltwhistle	7.31	9.10	Passenger (then shunts yard)
Alston	9.42	–	Light engine (to shed)

A comparison made between these timings and the public timetable quoted earlier will reveal that the 1.41 and 8.20 pm trains from Alston and the 12.35 and 6.20 pm departures from Haltwhistle were *not* worked by the Alston engine — these services were in fact worked by Carlisle-based locomotives which also worked the branch goods service. Two engines were involved in this complex pattern of operation, and although it would be inappropriate to chronicle the daily movements of both locomotives, the timings for 'Carlisle Engine No. 7' will show the extent to which these engines were involved in everyday Alston branch workings.

Carlisle No. 7 Engine — May 1939 (Weekdays)

	arrive	*depart*	*Notes*
	am	am	
Shed	–	5.05	Light engine
Carlisle Canal	–	5.20	
Haltwhistle	8.16	9.45	Class D Goods to Alston
		pm	
Alston	11.17	12.35	Passenger
	pm		
Haltwhistle	1.06	2.39	
Carlisle Canal	4.03	4.08	Light engine
Shed	4.13	–	

The 1920s and 1930s were a time of rising unemployment and political crisis, but in retrospect, those pre-war years have acquired an aura of nostalgia; it was still possible — for example — to ramble across unspoiled moors or stroll along quiet country roads that had not yet become blighted by noisy, smelly motor cars. J.B. Dawson knew the Alston area in the pre-war period, and he has contributed an interesting, first-hand description of his very first visit to Alston in the summer of 1926 or 1927:

> For the first 20 years of my life my home was the country station of Eastgate, on the Wear Valley Junction — Wearhead Branch, where my father was station master. During that period my interest was centred on that branch — however the road sign near my home ended with the words 'Alston 17 miles' and for a long time I had known that, only ten miles beyond the end of my own line at Wearhead, railways started again. That ten miles I knew was over some of the highest ground in the North of England (and without habitation) but having got a bicycle I decided, one Bank Holiday Monday, to cycle to Alston on what I thought would be a fine day . . . I reached the summit at Kilhope and left the bike at the other side of the road while I started to investigate a monument on the moor; looking back I could not see the bike for mist, but I eventually found my way back to the road and pressed on to Alston at slow speed as the rain which had started falling prevented the brakes from gripping properly.
>
> On arrival at Alston the station was soon located, with a train in the platform consisting of a 'G5' 0–4–4T and three coaches. I do not remember the engine number but took details of two of the coaches which were branded (in small plates above the running board) H'WHISTLE — ALSTON. The third coach was an LNER-built third which was in the set because of the holiday weekend. There was another locomotive sticking out of the shed which I think was a Fletcher 0–6–0. I do not remember more about that first trip apart from the fact that there was a snow plough on the siding near the signal box. I was anxious to get back to Wearhead where I could get on a train if I wanted to, and it was not until the early 1930s that I visited Alston again, on that occasion by train from Newcastle.

Mr Dawson recalled that the two brake composites allocated to Alston were occasionally strengthened by the addition of up to two extra vehicles, so that, at times of peak demand, the branch train could incorporate up to four coaches.

Featherstone Park, Coanwood and Slaggyford all lost their station masters during the LNER period, and indeed, Featherstone Park was designated a 'halt' in the Winter 1933 timetable (though the word halt had been dropped by 1939). The signal boxes at Featherstone and Slaggyford had been reduced to gate boxes by the early 1920s, and in consequence the single line was thereafter worked in three block sections, with the electric train tablet between Haltwhistle and Coanwood and from Lambley to Alston, and the train staff and ticket system on the intervening section between Coanwood and Lambley; up and down workings were able to pass at Coanwood or (by shunting) at Lambley, but there were no proper passing stations with up and down platforms for passenger traffic.

Tales of the Line

The Alston branch was an integral part of everyday life for well over a century, and it is hardly surprising that, in time, it became (in common with most other rural branch lines) the subject of jokes, legends and local folk lore. The line was, in a very real sense, a 'family' affair — many railwaymen and travellers being related to each other; regular passengers were addressed by their first names, and it was not unknown for trains to make special stops in order that people could alight near isolated farms and cottages. If sheep strayed onto the line, train crews would think nothing of stopping to herd the strays back into their fields — while in winter the railway became a vital means of communication in an otherwise remote and isolated moorland area.

Many people travelled regularly on the branch trains — the early morning 'school' trains being particularly useful. A unique atmosphere surrounded the special Saturdays-only late night service from Haltwhistle to Alston, which usually conveyed revellers home from pubs or other places of entertainment; in the 1930s, this service left the junction at 10.37 pm and reached Alston by 11.09 pm. Rivalries between young men from Alston and the intermediate stations would sometimes result in minor brawls — but, in pre-war days, such incidents seldom got out of hand, and local people do not recall trains being vandalised or people being seriously injured. These late night trains were also recognised places for courtship to take place, and this inevitably contributed to the well-remembered 'party' atmosphere that prevailed on the 10.37 pm (SO) from Haltwhistle!

A tale recounted by former railwaymen concerns a local recluse who was often seen walking along the railway between Alston and his cottage near Slaggyford. This gentleman was said to have been banned from the trains 'because he was so dirty', but he was otherwise harmless, and nobody really minded when he scoured the permanent way 'looking for bits of coal'. One day, however, he was involved in a near-miss on the line, and fearing that he might be killed the railway authorities called in the police to give him a warning about the dangers of trespass on railway property; the police accordingly paid a visit to the old man's home — and on entering they were surprised to see that every nook and crevice of every room was literally *full* of coal!

Mention of trespassing on the railway brings to mind the tale of a man who frequently took a 'short cut' across Lambley viaduct. He was eventually trapped on the narrow bridge by an oncoming train, and could only escape by climbing onto the parapet — a terrifying ordeal that must have cured his desire to walk across the viaduct! On another occasion, this same habitual trespasser was walking along the line near Glendue viaduct when he discovered that a large tree had been blown down across the track; he promptly returned to Lambley, from where he was able to give warning of the dangerous obstruction further down the line.

In the very early days, railways such as the Alston branch were regulated by Greenwich Mean Time rather than the 'local time' registered by church clocks, and for this reason country folk invariably set their watches with reference to passing trains. This practice persisted until the 20th century and farmer's wife Mrs Moone remembered that, at Softley Farm, they 'did not need a clock' because 'most activities were governed by the times of the trains'! Another local farmer — Mr Alan Tweddle of Bellister Haugh — confirmed that many country people set their clocks and watches by the trains. He remembered that when the '11.55 am Alston train left Haltwhistle it was time to leave work and go for lunch'. (He added that the trains always kept very good time in those far-off days before World War II.) Mr Tweddle also referred to the arrangements whereby water for the branch locomotives came from a supply at Broomhouse Farm (near the 1¼ mile post) and was then fed to the water tower at Haltwhistle via a pipe. It was said that when the platelayers wanted some overtime they would block the outlet to the tank — though this may have been merely a malicious rumour spread by the locomotive department!

Most travellers and local residents remember the Alston branch with affection as part of the background to their everyday lives, and it would be fitting to end this section by quoting former driver Alan Robinson; his recollections did not extend as far back as the 1930s, but his memories of travelling up and down the valley during the changing seasons sum up the appeal of the Alston branch:

> When you write the story of the branch remember the seasons: the spring, when the first lambs were in the fields and farm workers gave friendly waves; the summer when the embankments were a blaze of colour with primroses, cowslips and bluebells; and the autumn which was the most beautiful season of all. The branch line served the people well, and when we sit and talk of railways someone always says there never was a branch line like the Alston branch!

World War Two

On Sunday, 3rd September, 1939 a period of growing international tension culminated in the outbreak of war betweeen Britain and Germany. Experts had predicted that whole cities would be wiped out in a matter of days, but in the event the expected 'knock-out blow' did not materialise, and the first months of war were so quiet that people began to speak of a 'Phoney' war! The sudden and unexpected Fall of France in May 1940 led to renewed fears of a sustained German air offensive, and in anticipation of massive damage in urban centres such as London, Newcastle and Gateshead, the LNER dispersed many engines to rural locations in order to create a vital reserve pool of locomotives. Alston was one of these rural dispersal points, and by May 1940 six engines had arrived from Heaton, Gateshead and Rothbury. The newcomers included class 'D49' 4–4–0 No. 211 *The York & Ainsty*, class 'C7' 4–4–2 No. 2211, class 'D49' No. 362 *The Goathland*, and class 'G5s' 0–4–4Ts Nos. 1755, 1795 and 2086; the regular branch engine at that time was class 'J21' 0–6–0 No. 51.

The two 4–4–0s left Alston in November 1940, while the 4–4–2 was moved at about the same time; none of these engines are likely to have been used in normal service on the branch, but 'G5' 0–4–4T No. 2086 took its place alongside No. 51 in everyday service. Nos. 1755 and 1795 had, in the meantime, left Alston, leaving two engines in regular use on the branch. An upsurge in stone traffic (needed for aerodrome construction) resulted in a considerable amount of extra shunting, and for this reason a 'Y1' Sentinel shunter was stationed at Alston in 1941. The engine concerned was No. 106, and the running superintendent's records (formerly held at York) show that it arrived on 29th March, 1941 and went to Gateshead on 15th May, 1942.

Wartime conditions led to a revival of coal mining in the Alston area, and mines that, in normal conditions, would have been abandoned as totally uneconomic, experienced a revival during the early part of the war — 'Featherstone No. 6 Pit', for instance, was worked until 1941, while the Ayle Colliery (to the north of Alston) was worked during the first part of the war. These smaller collieries were ultimately forced to close by shortages of labour, but coal production was maintained at the much larger Lambley Colliery, which employed 70 miners and 10 surface workers in 1941. Fluorspar production was of even greater importance to the war effort, and this mineral was mined at Alston throughout the war years.

Coal, stone and fluorspar formed the bulk of the wartime goods traffic, and with petrol rationing strictly enforced, the railway also carried at least some additional passenger traffic between 1939 and 1945. There were several military or government establishments in the Alston area, notably a Ministry of Supply depot at Plenmeller and an army training camp near Featherstone. At the same time, the desolate moorlands of Cumberland, Westmorland and neighbouring counties were regarded as the ideal location for prisoner-of-war camps, and there was at least one such camp in the Featherstone area. In this context it is interesting to record that police forces and Home Guardsmen throughout north-western England were alerted when Oberleutnant Franz von Werra escaped from a neighbouring PoW camp in the Lake District on 7th October, 1940; he was soon recaptured, but the Oberleutnant eventually succeeded in escaping from a prison camp in Canada — no German prisoner ever escaped from England in World War II!

Wartime train services were maintained by the two Alston-based engines, 'G5' 0–4–4T No. 2086 working most of the passenger turns while 'J21' No. 51 operated the goods trains. Occasionally, a second 'G5' was needed for

Class 'A8', 4–6–2T, No. 2146 hurries along the branch near Featherstone Park. These impressive looking tank engines started life as NER class 'D' 4–4–4Ts, becoming LNER class 'H1' after the grouping; all were rebuilt with the 4–6–2T wheel arrangement, between 1931 and 1936. *Neville Stead Collection*

yard shunting at Alston, and in the summer of 1942 these duties were undertaken by No. 405 (which had replaced the Sentinel shunter). It was common practice, at that time, for the regular Alston goods engine to spend much of its time shunting at Haltwhistle, and to avoid unnecessary light engine movements this locomotive usually ran to and from the junction on a double-headed passenger working. At the end of the war, 'G5' 0–4–4T No. 2086 was still busily employed as the Alston passenger locomotive, but its former companion, 'J21' 0–6–0 No. 51, had been replaced as the Alston goods engine by sister engine No. 1122.

The end of the war was followed, in 1947, by one of the worst winters in living memory, and as usual, the Alston Moor area suffered severely during the great freeze. Despite efforts to keep the line free of snow drifts, the branch became inexorably blocked at Softley Farm (between Lambley and Slaggyford) and Mr S. Wright — who had worked at Alston as an engine driver since 1941 — recalled that he was sent out with a snow clearance train in an attempt to clear the line:

> I was the driver given the task of opening the line which had become blocked with snow. We picked up 200 German prisoners-of-war at Featherstone station at 2.30 pm, and managed to get just beyond Slaggyford station. We were then confronted with a wall of snow higher than the engine itself. The men cut snow until 2.30 am without even a warm drink.

The line was eventually cleared, but further problems ensued on 22nd March, 1947 when life-expired wooden sleepers disintegrated as the 2 pm passenger train approached Gilderdale viaduct, throwing the train onto its side. A few months later, on 31st December, 1947, the British railway system was nationalised by Mr Attlee's Labour Government, and the LNER era was thereby brought to a close.

HALTWHISTLE AND ALSTON.

Local Service see Table			WEEKDAYS		SX	SO		SO		SO
			a.m.	a.m.	a.m.	a.m.	p.m.	p.m.	p.m.	p.m.
134	York	dep.	3 45	7 15	11 30	11 30	1 25	....	3 35	6 43
134	Darlington	,,	4 51	9 0	12 21	12 21	1 36	..	4 27	8 28
194	Newcastle	,,	6 40	10 30	1 20	1T20	3 20	....	6 20	9 20
194	Carlisle	dep.	7 29	10 15	1 35	1 35	3 45	5 0	7 0	8 58
	HALTWHISTLE	dep.	8 10	11 50	2 34	2 43	4 46	6 15	7 45	10 37
	Featherstone Park	,,	8 18	11 58	2 42	2 51	4 54	6 23	7 53	10 45
	Coanwood	,,	8 22	12 2	2 46	2 55	4 58	6 27	7 57	10 49
	Lambley	,,	8 25	12 5	2 49	2 58	5 1	6 30	8 0	10 52
	Slaggyford	,,	8 33	12 13	2 57	3 6	5 9	6 38	8 8	11 0
	ALSTON	arr.	8 42	12 22	3 6	3 15	5 18	6 47	8 17	11 9

Local Service see Table			WEEKDAYS				SO		SO
			a.m.	a.m.	p.m.	p.m.	p.m.	p.m.	p.m.
	ALSTON	dep.	7 10	1010	1 41	3 55	5 30	6 55	9 10
	Slaggyford	,,	7 19	1019	1 50	4 4	5 39	7 4	9 19
	Lambley	,,	7 27	1027	1 58	4 12	5 47	7 12	9 27
	Coanwood	,,	7 30	1030	2 1	4 15	5 50	7 15	9 30
	Featherstone Park	,,	7 34	1034	2 5	4 19	5 54	7 19	9 34
	HALTWHISTLE	arr.	7 41	1041	2 12	4 26	6 1	7 26	9 41
194	Carlisle	arr.	8 39	1207	2 56	5 24	7 5	8 30	11 22
194	Newcastle	arr.	9 20	1157	4 0	6 2	..	8 32	10 59
134	Darlington	,,	1025	1 30	5 3	8F14	....	1038	12a12
134	York	,,	1135	2 18	5 52	9 15	..	12 0	1 10

D On Saturdays arrives Carlisle 11.26 a.m.
F On Saturdays arrives Darlington 7.11 p.m.
SO Saturdays only.
SX Saturdays excepted.
T Commencing 4th June leaves Newcastle 1.25 p.m.
a a.m.

LNER Spring 1938 passenger timetable.

Chapter Three

Along the Line; Haltwhistle to Slaggyford

Having described the history of the Alston branch from its inception until the Second World War, it would now be appropriate to examine the route and stations of this interesting line in greater detail. This chapter will therefore take readers on an imaginary journey over the branch from Haltwhistle to Alston; the topographical details will be correct for the 1950s or early 1960s, although for completeness some long-vanished features will also be mentioned.

Haltwhistle

Haltwhistle, the northernmost limit of operation for most branch passenger services, was a small but busy rural junction with staggered up and down platforms — the eastbound or up (i.e. Newcastle) platform being further east than its counterpart on the opposite side of the line; the westbound platform was an island with an outer face serving branch trains and allowing easy interchange for through travellers.

The main station building was on the eastbound side, and like other N&CR stations (and other NER stations) it was of Tudor-gothic design, and of considerable architectural merit. Nearby, a solid, two-storey station house provided suitable accommodation for the station master and his family; both buildings were of Newcastle & Carlisle origin, and probably dated from the opening of the line in 1838. Unusually, these original buildings were situated at track level,* access to the adjacent Newcastle platform being via the platform ramp. The platform itself was equipped with a wooden waiting room, and there was a similar structure on the Carlisle side of the line. The latter building had a stylish, half-hipped roof, and its timber walling incorporated an unusual 'herring bone' method of construction. The up and down platforms were linked by an ornate footbridge, and the station was controlled from a tall, NER-style signal cabin with a jetted upper storey and exposed point rodding.

Other facilities at Haltwhistle included a substantial stone goods shed, a 42 ft turntable for the branch engine, extensive goods and marshalling sidings, and some characteristic NER coal drops. Water columns were available on both platforms and in the tiny locomotive yard, while the goods yard was copiously-equipped with loading banks and docks. A particularly pleasing feature here were the wooden posted, ex-North Eastern Railway semaphore signals which survived for many years after the 1923 Grouping (the home signal at the western end of the station was a particularly good example — it was still *in situ* in the 1960s).

Haltwhistle itself could be seen to the north of the station; it was less than two miles from Hadrian's Wall, and the neighbourhood was dotted with castles and peel towers which served as poignant reminders of a turbulent and romantic past — a past punctuated by sudden raids and skirmishes, and peopled by larger-than-life characters such as 'Johnie Armstrang' and 'Kinmont Willie'! (men who would be 'Scottish when they will and English at their pleasure').

* None of the N&CR mainline stations had raised platforms, as originally built.

HALTWHISTLE. NER

A panoramic view of Haltwhistle station from the west. The Alston branch platform can be seen to the right, while the goods shed and yard are to the left; the period is *c*.1920. The 'zero' mileage post for the Alston Branch can be seen by the yard light in the middle foreground. *Lens of Sutton*

Haltwhistle with a Newcastle D.M.U. leaving on the 4th October, 1963. The footbridge is a standard cast-iron NER construction. The signal box was built in 1901 replacing the original 1870s bridge cabin to the west of the footbridge. *Oakwood Collection*

A fine view of the 1901 signal box at Haltwhistle station showing the beautiful and distinctive lines of its construction. Note the wooden platform on the left, for the table exchange used for the Alston Branch. *N.E. Stead Collection*

The 15,000 gallon water tank supplied by R. Whyllis & Co. 1861 (*NER records*), now a grade II listed building, photographed in October 1963. *Oakwood Collection*

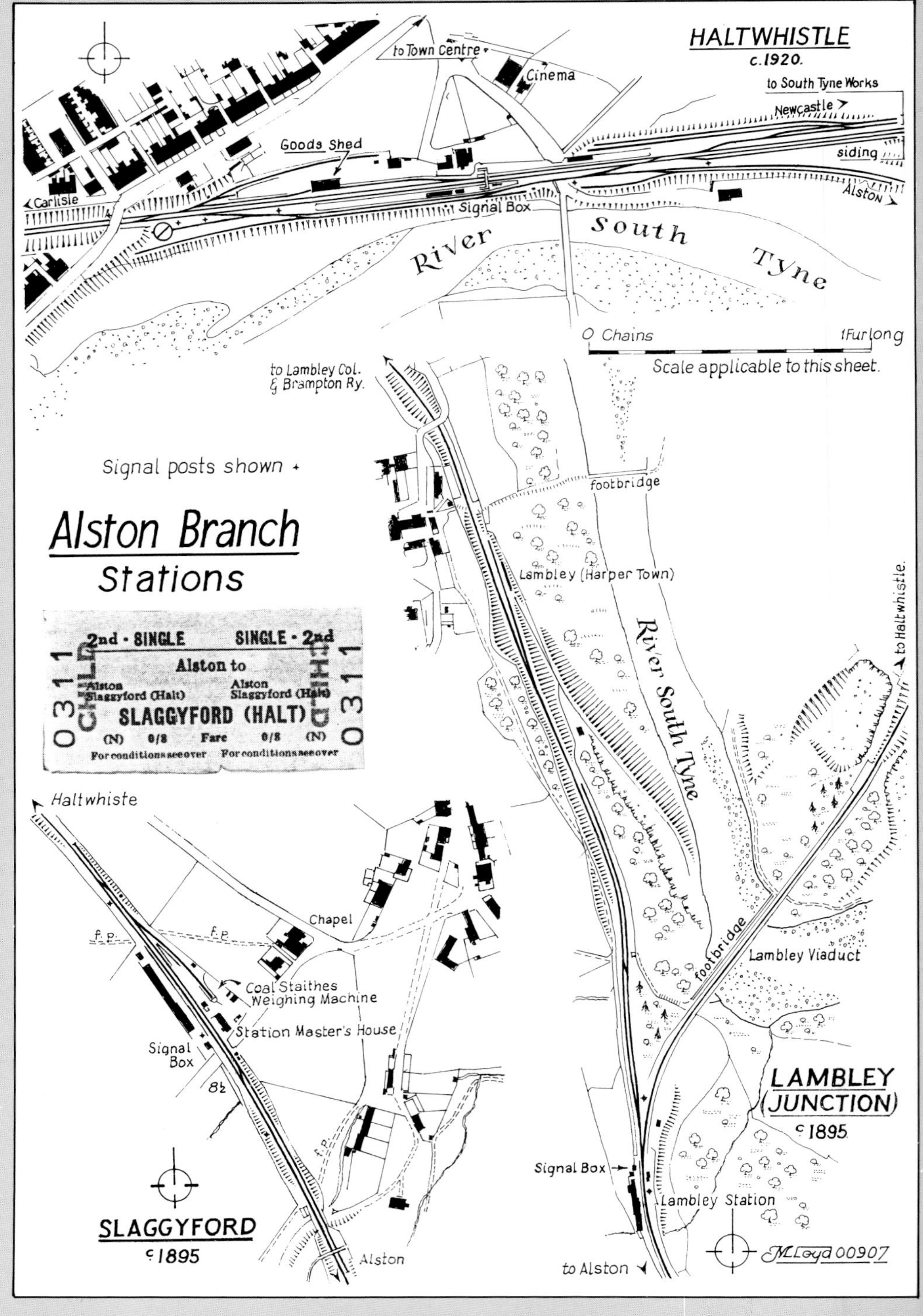
HALTWHISTLE
c.1920.
to Town Centre
Cinema
to South Tyne Works
Newcastle
Goods Shed
siding
Carlisle
Signal Box
Alston
River South Tyne
0 Chains
1 Furlong
Scale applicable to this sheet.
to Lambley Col. & Brampton Ry.
Signal posts shown +
footbridge
Alston Branch
Stations
Lambley (Harper Town)
River South Tyne
to Haltwhistle
2nd - SINGLE
SINGLE - 2nd
0311
CHILD
Alston to
Alston
Slaggyford (Halt)
SLAGGYFORD (HALT)
(N) 0/8 Fare 0/8 (N)
For conditions see over
For conditions see over
Haltwhiste
Chapel
f.p.
Coal Staithes
Weighing Machine
Station Master's House
Signal Box
8½
footbridge
Lambley Viaduct
LAMBLEY (JUNCTION)
c 1895
Signal Box
Lambley Station
SLAGGYFORD
c 1895
Alston
to Alston
M.Loyd 00907

A general view of Haltwhistle station in the 1960s with the Alston Branch D.M.U. taking on passengers, before the 'off'. *N.E. Stead Collection*

A platform-end view at Haltwhistle station showing the Alston Branch climbing away from the main line and swinging right to climb over the River South Tyne viaduct. *N.E. Stead Collection*

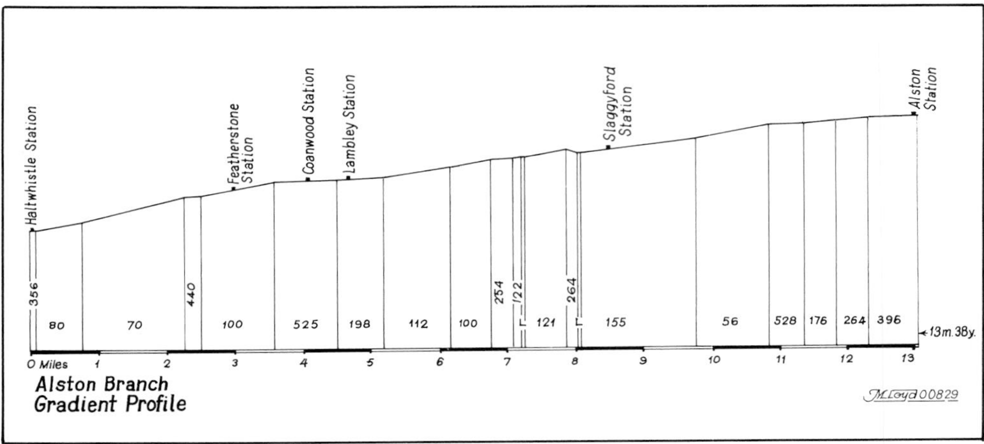

HALTWHISTLE and ALSTON.

Weekdays. **Sundays.**

Distance from Haltwhistle.	DOWN.	1	2	3	4	5	6	7	8		9	10	11	12	13	Sun. 1	Sun. 2	Sun. 3	Sun. 4
		WORKMEN'S TRAIN.	Empty Train.	WORKMEN'S TRAIN.	WORKMEN'S TRAIN.	Engine and Van.	B Goods and Mineral.	PASSENGER.	D Goods.			PASSENGER.	PASSENGER.	PASSENGER.	PASSENGER.				
		S O	MO	MS X	S O	Q	TSX Q							SX	S O				
									arr.	dep.									
		KZ		Z	PZ	BE	FJ			G									
M.C.		a.m.	a.m.	a.m.	a.m.	a.m.	a.m.	a.m.	a.m	a.m.		a.m.	p.m.	p.m.	p.m.				
.....	**Haltwhistle**	3 25	3 55	3 55	3 55	...	7 4*	8 5	9 32	10 36		11 45	4 20	8 0	8 15				
0 67	Plenmeller Halt	3 30		4 0	4 0	...	...	..	..	..		Y	..	..	..				
3 0	Featherstone Park					...	...	8 14	10 48	10 52		11 54	4 29	8 9	8 24				
4 8	Coanwood	3 41		4 11	4 11	..	..	8 18	11 1	11 24		11 58	4 33	8 13	8 28				
4 56	Lambley	3 41	...	4 14	4 14	...	...	8 21	11*28	12 22		12 1	4 36	8 16	8 31				
8 41	Slaggyford	5 51	...	4 21	4 24	...	...	8 30	12 34	12 52		12 10	4 45	8 2[illegible]	8 40				
13 0	**Alston**	4 4	4 25	4 34	4 34	6 10	8 22	8 40	1 4	—		12 20	4 55	8 35	8 50				

Weekdays. **Sundays.**

Distance from Alston.	UP.	1	2	3	4	5	6	7	8	9	10	11		12	13	Sun. 1	Sun. 2	Sun. 3	Sun. 4
		WORKMEN'S TRAIN.	Empty Train.	WORKMEN'S TRAIN.	D Cattle.		PASSENGER.	B Cattle.	PASSENGER.		PASSENGER.	D Goods.		PASSENGER.	PASSENGER.				
		S O	S O	SX	Q			SQ						S O	SX				
												arr.	dep.						
		KZ	P	Z	BL			J					NV						
M.C.		a.m.	a.m.	a.m.	a.m.		a.m.	a.m.	a.m.		p.m.	p.m.	p.m.	p.m.	p.m.				
.....	**Alston**	2 10	3 0	3 10	6 45		7 5	9 35	10 0		1 55	—	2 5	6 55	6 55				
4 39	Slaggyford	2 20	..	3 20	..		7 15	..	10 10		2 5	2 20	2 30	7 5	7 5				
8 24	Lambley	2 29	....	3 29	....		7 24	....	10 19		2 14	2 43	2 55	7 14	7 11				
8 72	Coanwood	2 32	..	3 32	..		7 27	..	10 22		2 17	3 0	3 10	7 17	7 17				
10 0	Featherstone Park	2 36	....	3 36	7 b 16		7 31	10 b 5	10 26		2 21	3 15	3 25	7 21	7 21				
12 13	Plenmeller Halt	2 47	..	3 47	..		..	..	..		..	..	..	..	7 29				
13 0	**Haltwhistle**	2 50	3 35	3 50	7 25		7 40	10 15	10 35		2 30	3 40	4 25	7 30	7 32				

B—Branch stations to advise station master, Alston, when they have traffic, and he will transmit the information to the Yard Master, Carlisle, specially stating when the train is required on the branch. In the latter case he will advise the station master Haltwhistle, who will arrange staff working. b—Brakes. E—Carlisle dep. 4.45 a.m., p. 147. F—Carlisle dep. 5.35 a.m., p. 147. G—Carlisle dep. 8.15 a.m., p. 148. J—Runs in connection with Haltwhistle Stock Sales. K—Runs on 16th July and alternate Saturdays following. L—Carlisle arr. 9.29 a.m., p. 142. N—Barrhaugh Siding A, Armstrong's Siding 2.47–2.57. P—Runs on 23rd July and alternate Saturdays following. V—Blaydon Sidings arr. 8.6 p.m., p. 150. Y—Stops on 22nd July and on alternate Fridays following to pick up workmen. Z—Empty train between Haltwhistle and Plenmeller Halt.

NER working timetable for the Branch dated July 1921.

Like other country stations, Haltwhistle was a significant employment centre in a mainly rural area, and several railwaymen lived in the town or in railway cottages near the goods yard. Haltwhistle's station master was a figure of some importance in this tightly-knit community, and in the 1880s this prestigious position was filled by William Arthur; a later station master was John Austin, who was in charge during the Edwardian period.

Alston branch trains departed from the southernmost of Haltwhistle's three platform faces and ran eastwards for a short distance before diverging abruptly south-eastwards onto the single track branch. Climbing at 1 in 80, the line curved southwards in a great arc which took it through a full 90 degree turn before trains crossed the sparkling South Tyne for the first time on a graceful arched viaduct — the first of many on this heavily-engineered scenic route. The South Tyne viaduct had a 29 ft square span and five 53 ft skew spans; its central piers were pierced by lateral arches and strengthened by prominent tri-angular buttresses.

Having reached the south bank of the river trains ran south-west on a high embankment that was pierced, at one point, by an underbridge with a 22 ft skew span. Beyond, the single line entered a substantial cutting as it meandered south-westwards for the first part of its run down the South Tyne valley.

Plenmeller Colliery and Halt

Passing beneath an arched stone occupation bridge, southbound trains reached the site of Plenmeller Colliery Halt (79 chains). The history of this little known industrial site is surprisingly complex, and it would appear that three separate seams were worked at various times; the first shaft was in use by 1847, and this initial shaft remained in operation until May 1903 when the 'Cannel' seam became exhausted. Other seams continued to be worked, and National Coal Board records reveal that a drift mine was in operation at that time. In 1909 Plenmeller Collieries Ltd arranged with the NER for a private siding to be installed near the pit, and in June 1919 a new halt was opened to cater for miners working in the colliery.

The colliery platform was situated on the down side of the line, and miners had to cross the nearby exchange sidings in order to reach the pit head — although it is possible that one of the colliery's own locomotives could have been used to work a miners' shuttle service to and from the main line platform. The halt itself was a simple, earth-and-sleeper platform, and entry to the colliery exchange sidings was controlled by a ground frame.

Although Plenmeller Colliery sidings were installed in 1909, full-scale coal extraction did not commence until several years later, and in 1910 the mine employed only 39 men underground and 49 above. A new, deep level shaft was at that time still being sunk, and the associated pit head winding gear was not erected until 1914. Interestingly, the Plenmeller Colliery Company decided that instead of conventional steam driven winding equipment, their new shaft would be worked on the innovative 'Koepe' system, whereby the familiar colliery winding drum would be replaced by a simple rope-and-pulley arrangement. As heavy steam driven equipment

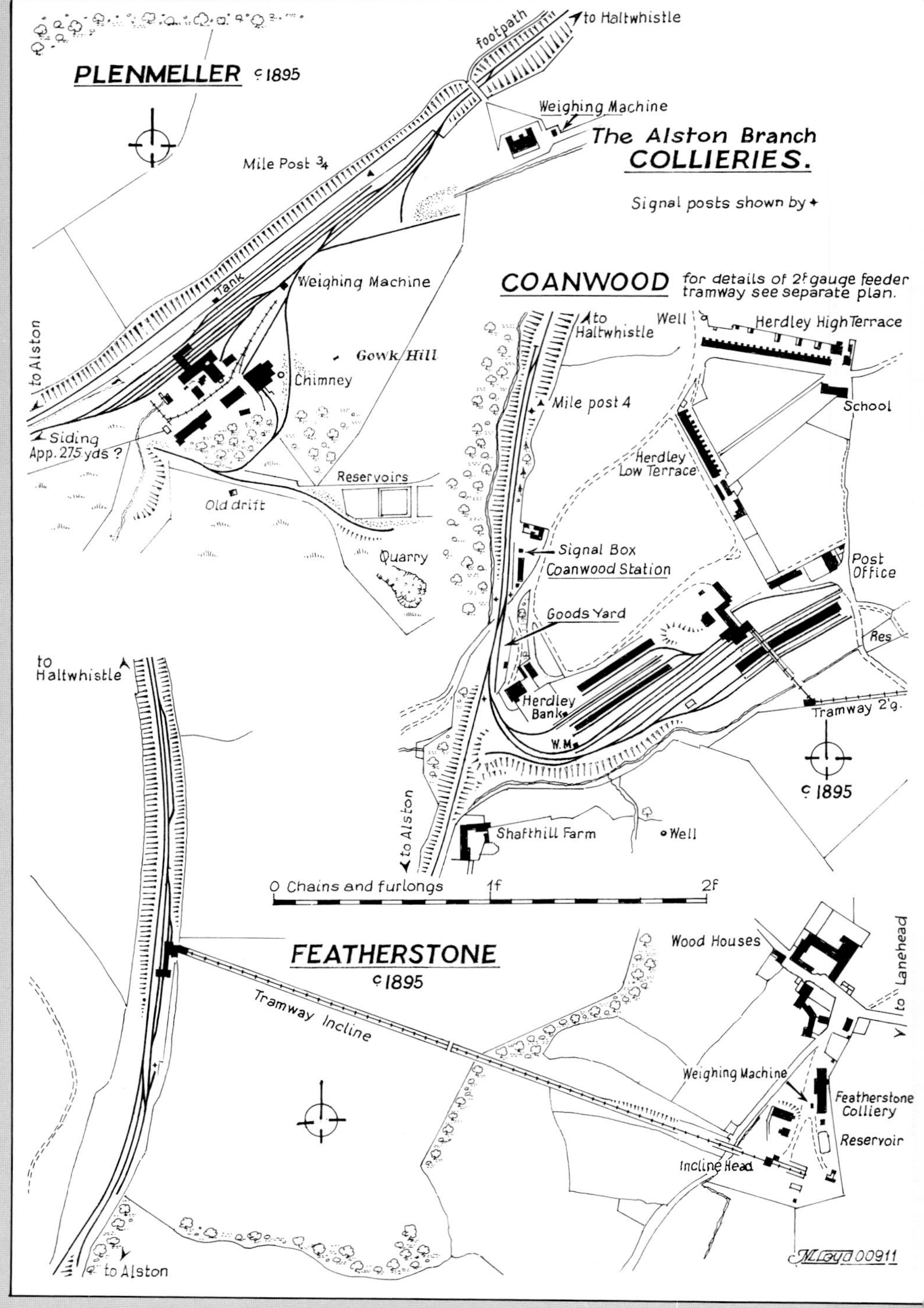
The Alston Branch
COLLIERIES.
Signal posts shown by ✦
PLENMELLER c1895
to Haltwhistle
footpath
Weighing Machine
Mile Post 3/4
Weighing Machine
Tank
Gowk Hill
Chimney
to Alston
Siding
App. 275 yds ?
Reservoirs
Old drift
Quarry
COANWOOD
for details of 2ft gauge feeder tramway see separate plan.
to Haltwhistle
Well
Herdley High Terrace
School
Mile post 4
Herdley
Low Terrace
Signal Box
Coanwood Station
Post
Office
Goods Yard
Res
Herdley
Bank
W.M.
Tramway 2'g.
c1895
to Alston
Shafthill Farm
Well
0 Chains and furlongs
1f
2f
to
Haltwhistle
FEATHERSTONE
c1895
Tramway Incline
Wood Houses
to Lanehead
Weighing Machine
Featherstone
Colliery
Reservoir
Incline Head
to Alston
M.Lloyd 00911

A fine view of Plenmeller Colliery in the 1920s. *Courtesy P. Lefevre*

Locomotive No. 3 built 1887 seen here in a derelict state at Plenmeller Colliery in July 1932 after closure of colliery. *F. Jones Collection*

would have been unsuitable, the Koepe winding hoist was powered by a direct current electric motor, the whole assembly being mounted in a huge steel tower.

The use of this German-designed system attracted much attention at the time of its installation, and in 1918 the following description of the plant was printed in the *Transactions of the Institution of Mining Engineers*:

> The contract was placed with the British Westinghouse Electric & Manufacturing Company Limited in March 1910, but the erection of the plant was only commenced in June 1914, and it was not put into operation until May 1916. These delays were principally due to protracted sinking difficulties . . . The structural portion of the tower was sublet by the British Westinghouse Company to the Teeside Bridge & Engineering Works, Middlesborough, and the mechanical equipment to Messrs Cowans Sheldon & Company Limited, Carlisle. The equipment was designed for the following duty: winding depth, 800 feet; coal per wind, 45 cwt; winding time, 45 seconds; decking time, 25 seconds. The actual winding depth is 815 feet and the coal drawn per wind 48 cwt.
>
> The structure is built up principally of steel joists braced together against the winding and wind-pressure stresses. The overall height of the structure is 84 feet 8 inches, the banking out level being carried at 22¾ feet from the ground or shaft-collar level, the first floor of the engine house at 56 feet 7 inches and the second floor at 66 feet 7 inches. A cast iron spiral staircase is provided between the ground level and the second (engine house) level floor, with off-sets at the bank level and the first engine house floor level. The whole structure is of steel, and is covered in by galvanised corrugated sheeting.
>
> The upper or second engine house floor carries the direct-current winding motor and driving pulley, and the lower or first floor the guide-pulley, motor generator set, switchboard, driver's platform, controller, etc. The eight guide ropes are held by Reliance glands carried by the first floor of the engine house . . . the winding motor, which is rated at 240 horse power (and designed by means of the Ward-Leonard control for any speed between 'creeping' and 200 revolutions per minute) is operated in conjunction with the motor generator set, which latter consists of a 200-kilowatt 350-volt direct-current generator, driven by a 600-volt three-phase 50 period induction motor at 730 revolutions per minute, with an exciter running on the same shaft.

Among the many advantages that were expected to accrue from the employment of the Koepe system were high efficiency, low maintenance, compactness, and relatively low initial costs. The plant was started-up in May 1916, and for the next few years the prominent Koepe winding tower stood at the centre of a thriving and comparatively large pit. By 1925 (when the pit was probably at its peak in terms of production and numbers of men employed) Plenmeller Colliery was providing work for 292 underground and 80 surface workers — many of whom travelled daily to work on the adjacent railway. Five years later, the total numbers of employees at Plenmeller had dropped to 337, but the pit remained an important employment centre until its ultimate closure in 1932.

Prior to its demise, the Plenmeller Colliery had owned three small 0–4–0 saddle tanks, one of which had seen earlier service on the London & South Western Railway, while another had originally worked at a chemical works.

Plenmeller sidings were re-opened by the Ministry of Supply in the early months of World War II, and LNER working appendices show that the

Featherstone Park station, looking north towards Haltwhistle on 30th June, 1956. The goods loop and sidings had been lifted following the withdrawal of goods facilities in August 1954, but the abandoned cattle dock and coal drops can be seen to the right. *P.B. Booth*

A closer view of Featherstone Park station on 4th October, 1963, showing the slotted post NER signal which survived for many years as the up home. The gable-roofed storage building immediately behind the signal was probably the old signal cabin, which was taken out of use around 1904, after the opening of the later hipped-roof box. *Oakwood Collection*

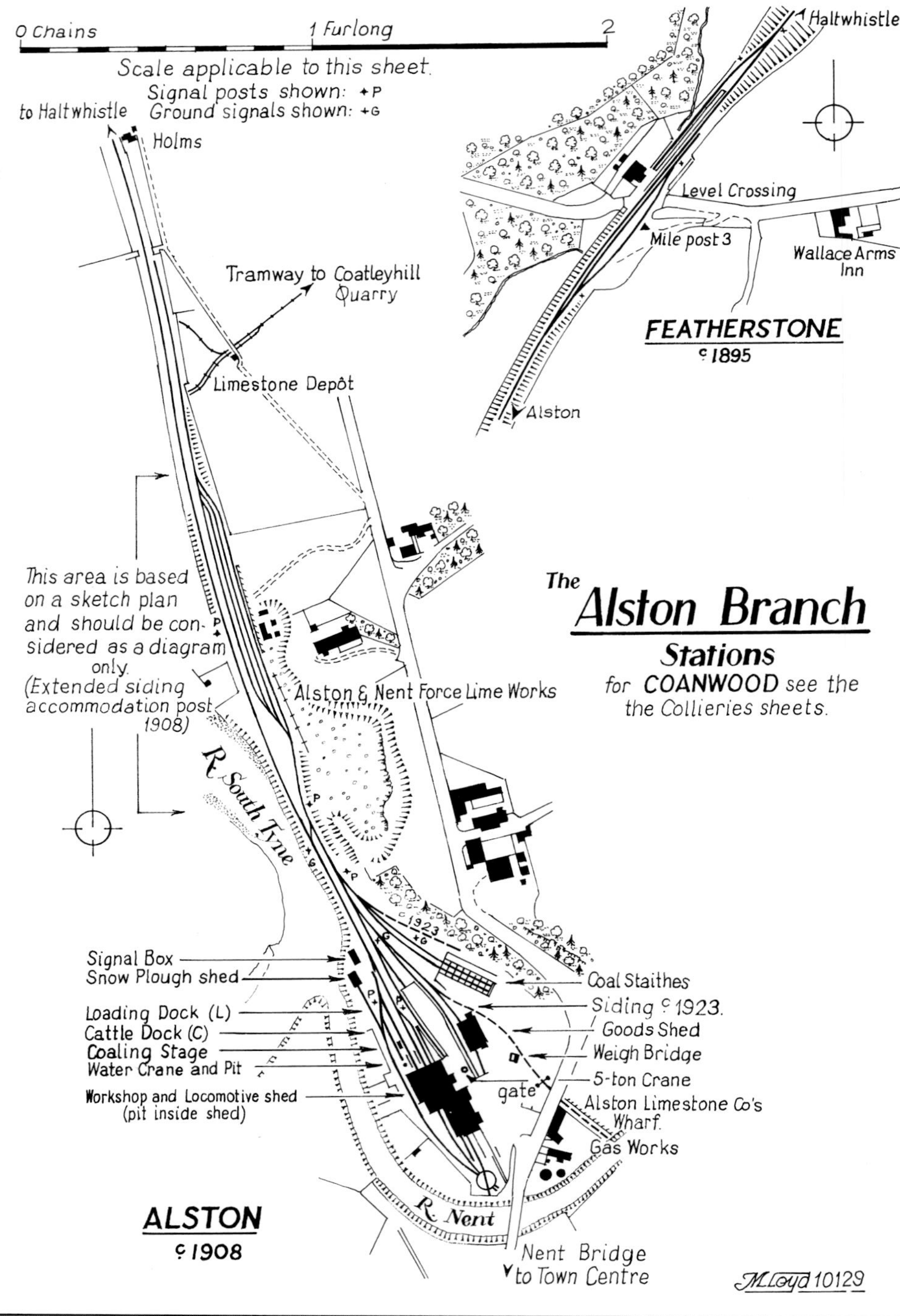

0 Chains
1 Furlong
2
Scale applicable to this sheet.
Signal posts shown: +P
Ground signals shown: +G
to Haltwhistle
Holms
Tramway to Coatleyhill Quarry
Limestone Depôt
This area is based on a sketch plan and should be considered as a diagram only.
(Extended siding accommodation post 1908)
Alston & Nent Force Lime Works
R. South Tyne
1923
Signal Box
Snow Plough shed
Loading Dock (L)
Cattle Dock (C)
Coaling Stage
Water Crane and Pit
Workshop and Locomotive shed (pit inside shed)
Coal Staithes
Siding c 1923.
Goods Shed
Weigh Bridge
5-ton Crane
gate
Alston Limestone Co's Wharf.
Gas Works
R. Nent
Nent Bridge
to Town Centre
ALSTON
c 1908
Haltwhistle
Level Crossing
Mile post 3
Wallace Arms Inn
FEATHERSTONE
c 1895
Alston
The Alston Branch
Stations
for COANWOOD see the the Collieries sheets.
M.Lloyd 10129

connection from the single line was unlocked by the electric train tablet which had recently been introduced between Haltwhistle and Coanwood. Locomotives were permitted to propel wagons from Haltwhistle to Plenmeller, provided that the engine was always at the Haltwhistle end of the train (to reduce the risk of breakaways on the steep gradients between Haltwhistle and the sidings). Having picked-up loaded wagons from the colliery sidings, trains could return to the junction provided that the guard first obtained permission by telephoning the signal box at Haltwhistle.

Plenmeller sidings remained *in situ* in the post-war period, and observant travellers were able to discern an array of exchange sidings on the left hand side of the main line as their train clattered past Plenmeller Ground Frame; the sidings were finally lifted in the mid-1960s, but the site had, by that time, been cleared to make way for modern industrial development.

Featherstone Park

With patches of open moorland visible on all sides, trains climbed towards Featherstone Park on a 1 in 70 rising gradient, which eventually eased to 1 in 100 as the route traversed a lengthy stretch of cuttings. There, were several overbridges on this section, among them an arched occupation bridge at 1 mile 43 chains and a timber footbridge at 1 mile 51 chains; both of these structures were wide enough to accommodate a double track, the former having a skew span of 29 ft 7 in. while the footbridge had a span of 25 ft. A third bridge, at 1 mile 58 chains, had a single stone arch with a span of 25 ft 3 in. These three structures were numbered consecutively from 6 to 8 in the Alston branch bridge-numbering sequence.

Still in cuttings, the railway continued south-westwards as it ran past the small hamlet of Park; the public road from Park to Rowfoot was carried over the line on a single-span stone bridge. Crossing Park Burn by means of a single-span underline culvert (bridge 10), down trains reached the intermediate station at Featherstone Park. This small stopping place was 3 miles 7 chains from Haltwhistle, and it served the inhabitants of Rowfoot - a small hamlet to the east of the railway. The station was originally called 'Featherstone', but the name was later changed to Featherstone Park (presumably to prevent confusion with a Lancashire & Yorkshire Railway station at Featherstone, near Leeds).

Like other stations on the Alston branch, Featherstone Park had only one platform. Its modest track layout incorporated a loop siding with an intermediate crossover to facilitate shunting operations; the total length of the loop siding was about 10.49 chains. The 260 ft passenger platform was on the up side, and the goods loop was on the down side of the line. A minor road crossed the line on the level at the south end of the platform.

The station had once been a block post, but the loop was not signalled for crossing purposes, and although a standard North Eastern-style hipped-roof signal cabin was provided, it was used as a 'gate box' rather than a signal box. The box, which was sited immediately to the south of the platform on the up side, was of brick construction, and it measured approximately 17 ft x 13½ ft at ground level.

Short sidings diverged from both the up and down sides, the main goods siding being to the rear of the platform on the up side, while a separate coal siding was situated on the down side. The latter siding was equipped with coal drops, while a cattle dock with a 52 ft loading platform was sited alongside the main loop siding. There was provision for general merchandise traffic, although the cattle dock and a 2-ton yard crane had been removed by the late 1920s. Entry to the goods sidings was controlled from a frame released by the Haltwhistle-Coanwood electric train tablet, and the level crossing gates were worked by a wheel.

The station building was a two-storey, cottage style structure incorporating domestic accommodation for the station master and his family. The main block was at right angles to the platform, while smaller wings extended from both sides of this attractive stone-built structure. The building material was coursed stonework, and minor details included a projecting bay window at the front of the building, and ornate Tudor-style chimney stacks.

It is sometimes said that Featherstone Park and the other Alston branch stations were built in the so-called 'Jacobean' style of 17th century architecture, but in reality their period details reflected Elizabethan rather than Jacobean practice, the flamboyant curved gables that would normally have been found on Jacobean buildings being entirely absent. Featherstone Park had the smallest and simplest station building *en route* to Alston, although it was clearly in the same architectural family as its counterparts elsewhere on the line.

Minor details at this remote country station included a small gable roofed building on the up side of the line beside the level crossing. From its appearance, this ramshackle structure once served as a signal cabin, though it became a storage shed after the new brick signal box was built around 1904. The level crossing was protected by semaphore signals in each direction, one of these being an up home, while the other (on the north side of the crossing) was a down starting signal. The platform was fenced with vertical wooden paling, while at night the station was illuminated by simple oil lamps in tapering glass lanterns.

In NER days Featherstone Park had been important enough to have its own station master, and successive editions of *Kelly's Directories* record many of their names. In 1886, for instance, the station was supervised by James Kirton, while in 1914 the station master was John Sharp. In later years the station was down-graded to become little more than a halt.

From 1932 until 1940 no money was taken at Featherstone Park; instead, local travellers were issued with 'check tickets', the actual fares being collected at Haltwhistle or intermediate stations to Alston. The staff complement was, by that time, just two porter-signalmen, who were needed to operate the crossing gates and carry out station duties.

Peter Huntsman, who worked as a guard on the Alston branch after World War II, recalled that when he started work on the line the Featherstone Park crossing keeper - Mrs S.E. Armstrong - would always leave a flask of tea on the station seat at 6.30 am each morning in order that the crew of the first down train could have a warming drink; this was of course much appreciated during the harsh Northumberland winters!

Featherstone Park was not, by any stretch of the imagination, a busy place, although it handled a heavy traffic in World War I, when a military camp was established in the area. A similar situation pertained in World War II, when an army camp was set up in the grounds of nearby Featherstone Castle. The camp was initially used as a training site for American military personnel, who called it 'Death Valley'. Later, as mentioned in Chapter Two, it became a prisoner-of-war camp, the idea being that the, utter remoteness of the surrounding area would discourage potential escapees.

Such isolation made Featherstone Park an ideal refuge for the Royal Train, and in this context local people recall that King George VI's train was berthed at Featherstone during a royal tour of Tyneside. The royal visit was, in theory at least a 'secret', but security precautions were so conspicuous that the whereabouts of the royal special soon became common knowledge! The branch was closed to normal traffic, and soldiers were stationed on nearby bridges and at various other places around the royal train.

Reverting to Featherstone Park's role as a prisoner-of-war camp, it should perhaps be explained that very large numbers of German soldiers surrendered to the British army at the end of World War II, so that they would not have to face the vengeance of the Russians. Featherstone Park Camp, which had housed Italian prisoners following the departure of the Americans, became a camp for German officers in 1945, and it remained in use for about three years. At its peak, the camp contained up to 4,000 prisoners, who were housed in four compounds surrounded by watch towers and barbed wire fences. Most of the camp buildings were Nissen huts.

As 're-education' continued, the barbed wire was removed and the prisoners were allowed out on parole. Cultural activities flourished within the camp, and the inmates were encouraged to form an orchestra and run their own radio station and newspaper. Featherstone Park PoW Camp was closed in 1948, but its name lived on in the form of the 'Featherstone Park Group', which was formed to promote Anglo-German friendship and reconciliation.

Featherstone Park lost its goods facilities during the early part of the BR era, the goods yard being closed with effect from 23rd August, 1954. All sidings and connections were then lifted, although the abandoned cattle dock and coal drops could be seen alongside the running line for many years thereafter.

Leaving Featherstone Park trains passed over the road from Rowfoot to Featherstone Castle, and, still climbing at 1 in 100, the scenic journey to Alston resumed. Running first on embankments, and then in cuttings, the railway headed more or less due south through pleasant Northumberland scenery. Bridge 13, at 3 miles 49 chains, was similar to its counterparts elsewhere on the line, with a 25 ft 4 in. single span that was clearly designed to accommodate a second line of rails. Beyond, the route levelled off, and falling imperceptibly at 1 in 525, down trains reached the site of Featherstone Colliery Sidings.

Featherstone Colliery

Featherstone Colliery was situated about half a mile to the east of the railway, and like Plenmeller Colliery, its history was somewhat chequered. The colliery was one of a group owned by Lord Carlisle and worked during the 19th century by Charles Thomas Lacy Thompson (1857-1920). National Coal

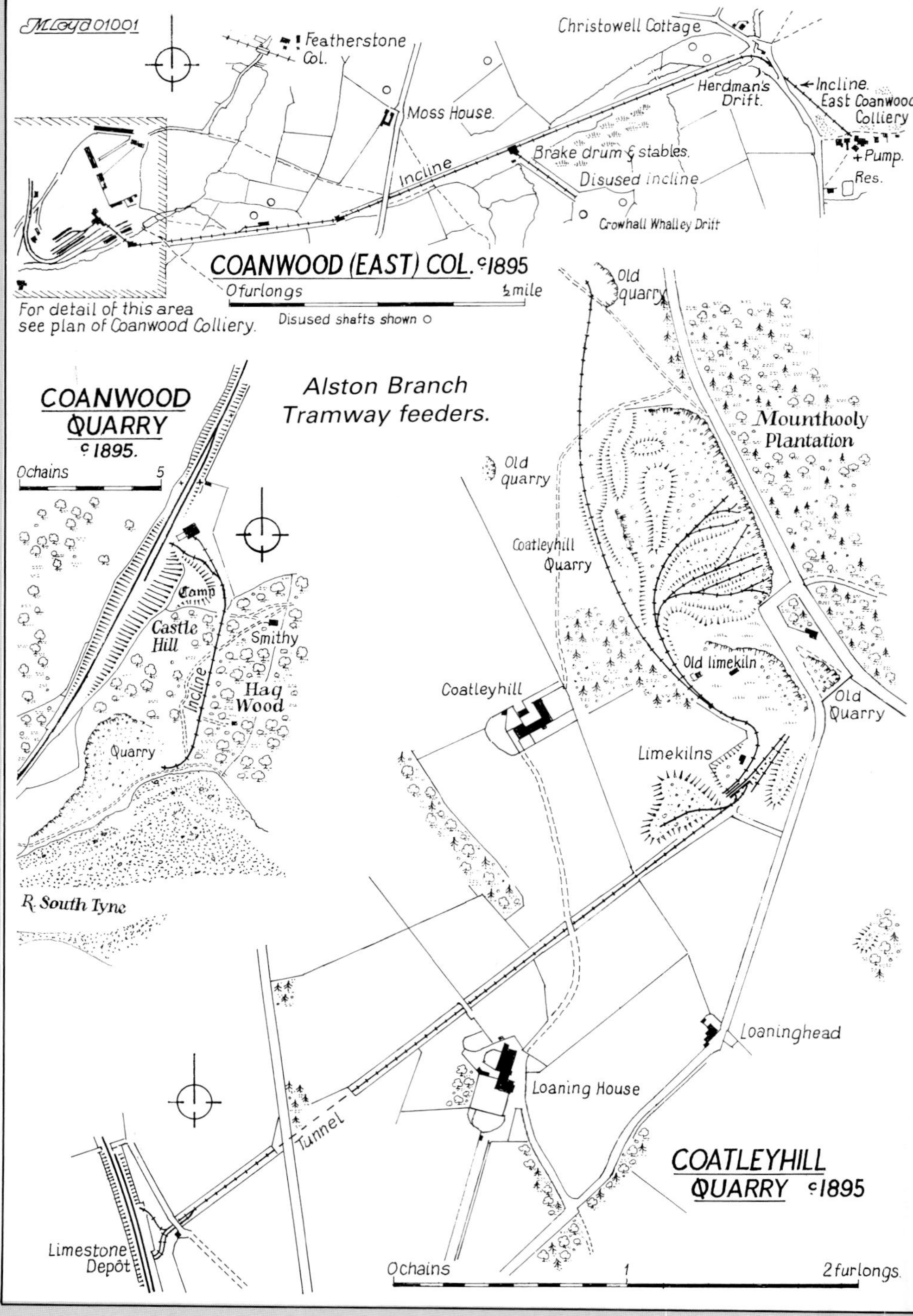

MLloyd 01001
Featherstone Col.
Moss House.
Christowell Cottage
Herdman's Drift.
Incline.
East Coanwood Colliery
Pump.
Res.
Incline
Brake drum & stables.
Disused incline
Crowhall Whalley Drift
COANWOOD (EAST) COL. c1895
0 furlongs
½ mile
For detail of this area see plan of Coanwood Colliery.
Disused shafts shown o
COANWOOD QUARRY c1895.
0 chains
5
Alston Branch Tramway feeders.
Camp
Castle Hill
Smithy
Incline
Hag Wood
Quarry
R. South Tyne
Old quarry
Old quarry
Mounthooly Plantation
Coatleyhill Quarry
Old limekiln
Coatleyhill
Old Quarry
Limekilns
Loaninghead
Loaning House
Tunnel
Limestone Depôt
COATLEYHILL QUARRY c1895
0 chains
1
2 furlongs.

Close-up of the simple wooden station building at Coanwood; erected in 1877–78, the station cost £672. The standard NER signal box can be glimpsed in the background with the slotted post signal missing the home arm. *P.B. Booth*

Coanwood station at the end of its days. Only the small wooden shelter remains, the white railings replacing the open wooden shelter and rooms. *Oakwood Collection*

Board records show that the main seam was exhausted by January 1905, but a small group of working miners later re-entered the pit and commenced taking out the pillars of coal that had been left in place by the bigger colliery companies; these miners continued their small scale operations for about 12 years, and they also worked various small drift mines in the surrounding hills — thereby continuing a tradition of rural mining that dated back to the Middle Ages.

In its heyday, Featherstone Colliery must have been a relatively large-scale pit, and the exchange sidings between Featherstone Park and Coanwood stations were surprisingly complex. Large scale Ordnance Survey maps show an array of parallel loops and reception sidings, together with a structure which may have been a screening plant. The reception sidings were linked to the pithead complex by an inclined plain that extended eastwards for approximately half a mile.

Featherstone Colliery Siding was mentioned in the 1904 *Railway Clearing House Handbook of Stations*, but this facility was subsequently taken out of use, and in later years the abandoned site was marked only by a retaining wall on the east side of the railway.

Coanwood

Continuing southwards, trains ran through a succession of cuttings and embankments as they approached Coanwood, the next stopping place *en route* to Alston. Situated some 4 miles 18 chains from Haltwhistle, Coanwood was a small station serving nearby coal mining and quarrying communities — Coanwood Colliery being more or less adjacent to the railway, while Coanwood Whinstone Quarry was only half a mile further on.

In operational terms, Coanwood was of some importance in that it marked the end of the first block section, the line north to Haltwhistle being worked by electric train tablet, while the section south to Lambley was operated on the older, 'staff and ticket' system, whereby a series of trains could proceed onto the single line provided that their respective drivers possessed written authorisation in lieu of a train staff; the staff itself would be carried by the very last train in an up or down series.

Coanwood's importance was underlined by the fact that, alone among stations on the Alston branch, it had once boasted a lengthy crossing loop. However, there was just one 250 ft platform on the down side of the line, and this meant that the station was not suited for passing two passenger trains (there were, on the other hand, few problems if the need arose to pass a passenger train and a freight working). Like Featherstone Park, Coanwood was bisected by a level crossing which effectively divided the station into two — the passenger platform being to the north while the tiny goods yard was on the south side of the crossing gates. The yard was equipped to handle coal, cattle and general merchandise traffic and a small hand crane was available for use when timber, drain pipes or other large items were consigned by rail.

As we have seen, Coanwood was not an original station, and although the temporary stopping place known as 'Shafthill' had been situated in the immediate vicinity, a permanent station did not appear until 1877–78.

Known as Shafthill until 1885, Coanwood had simple wooden station buildings with a recessed central portion which formed an open-fronted waiting area or *loggia* for potential travellers; doors gave access to a booking office and other facilities, and the whole structure was painted in LNER style green and cream paint (in earlier years the building had probably been painted in contrasting shades of brown and light stone).

Other buildings at Coanwood included a small wooden storage shed beside the station building, a signal cabin, and the station master's house. The signal box was originally sited to the north of the station building, but this structure (which must have been a very small platform box) was replaced around 1904 when the North Eastern Railway erected a two-storey, hip-roofed box on a brick base. The new cabin was of typical NER Northern Division design, its overall appearance being very similar to the boxes at Alston, Lambley, Slaggyford and Featherstone Park.

Staffing arrangements at Coanwood echoed those at Featherstone Park, the underlying theme being one of rationalisation as the LNER sought ways of reducing expenditure at these remote and little-used outposts. Once considered important enough to have its own station master, Coanwood was latterly worked by just two porter-signalmen who carried out all station duties. In earlier, more prosperous days, the station had been supervised by station masters such as Rayson Cockton, who worked at Coanwood during the 1880s; a later station master, around 1912–14, was Mr Albert Hope.

Coanwood Colliery

Coanwood Colliery Sidings (4 miles 22 chains) were entered via a facing connection at the Alston end of the station. Facilities here were both extensive and complex, and in addition to the usual screening and washing plants, a battery of coke ovens was also provided. The standard gauge sidings fanned out into 11 loading or marshalling sidings, while a 2 ft gauge tramway ran from the coke ovens to Crystal Well Drift and other nearby pits; local people recall that the 2 ft gauge line incorporated an incline, on which loaded tubs were used to pull the empties up by gravity. There were, as well as these surface lines, further tramways below ground, and pit ponies were used to haul colliery tubs along the underground roadways; hay from nearby Dykes meadows was used to feed the ponies. On one sad occasion, some of the animals were drowned when a local burn overflowed and flooded the pit.

Coanwood Colliery predated the railway by several years, and at least one seam was being worked around 1780. Large scale operations began after the opening of the railway, a 442 ft shaft being sunk between November 1860 and July 1863. The 'Coom Roof', 'Yard' and 'Slag' seams were worked during the 19th century; these seams remained in operation until the 1890s, but the mine was abandoned in May 1894 after being 'drowned out in consequence of stoppage of pumping' at an adjoining colliery. Happily, this disaster was only temporary, and the Coanwood Coal Company was later able to resume coal extraction; the Yard, Coom Roof and other seams were finally abandoned at various times between 1904 and 1917.

The coke ovens ceased work around 1919, and the last of the chimneys at the coke plant were demolished with explosives in the next few months. This was not, however, the end of mining activity at Coanwood because F.G. Herdman & Co. of Newcastle continued to work smaller pits in the area to the east of Coanwood station. The 2 ft gauge tramway was retained for several years, but when Herdman & Co. started transporting coals to Coanwood station by road, the tramway fell into disuse (*see Chapter Six*).

Coanwood Whinstone Siding

From Coanwood the route continued southwards and, running on an embankment, trains passed over a farm track on an arched occupation bridge with a single span of 10 ft (bridge 15). Beyond, the line continued to the site of Coanwood Whinstone Siding — a short dead end siding on the down side. This facility served a nearby limestone quarry, an inclined plane being used to connect the siding to workings in the surrounding woods.

The Whinstone siding was inspected by Major-General Hutchinson of the Board of Trade on 15th September, 1894, and having passed its BoT inspection, it was soon handling significant quantities of locally-quarried stone. For a time, the Coanwood Whinstone Company's operations were modestly successful, and the quarry was employing some 47 men by 1897; this figure had risen to 55 within the next twelve months, and the quarry company had soon excavated a large hole between the railway embankment and the River South Tyne.

Unfortunately, the narrow wedge of land on which the quarry was situated did not permit expansion, either to the east or the west, and when it was discovered that the railway ran over a solid bed of valuable stone the NER (fearing, presumably, that continued quarrying would weaken the embankment) took legal action. Lengthy negotiations ensued, and in February 1914 the protagonists agreed that the railway company would pay compensation on a total of 115,452 tons of unworked stone that the quarry company would not be allowed to extract. At this juncture, Mr Hope Wallace, the owner of the land on which the quarry was situated, claimed 5*d*. a ton in respect of the disputed stone, and it was suggested that the railway company might pay him £2,196 to settle the matter; as the quarry company was also demanding £5,772, it appeared that the NER would have to pay almost £8,000. This figure was soon reduced to £3,600, but the dispute dragged on when Mr Hope Wallace refused to accept just £1,500. His obdurate response to the NER's offer succeeded only in damaging the unfortunate Whinstone Company, and quarrying operations had apparently ceased altogether by the outbreak of World War I.

Turning briefly to operational matters, it is interesting to find that although Coanwood Whinstone Siding was only a few chains beyond Coanwood station, it was fully protected by up and down signals, and as these were so close to the Coanwood up home and the Lambley down home, both carried fish-tailed distant arms. The siding was worked from a dwarf ground frame which, according to Major-General Hutchinson's BoT report, had six operational levers and two spares.

The Whinstone siding had been lifted by 1920, and once nature had hidden the scars of quarrying, there were few visible reminders of industrial

A fine view of Lambley junction with all its various sizes of NER slotted post signals. The Alston branch ran to the right while the colliery branch diverged to the left. The train in view is on the colliery branch. Note the two levels of the platform and the check-rails on the sharp curve. The viaduct is to the right of this photo.

N. Stead Collection

activity in this beautiful stretch of the South Tyne Valley. (Edwardian post cards show the quarry as a livid scar beside Lambley Viaduct, but within a few years the quarry face had weathered to such an extent that it resembled a natural cliff behind its screen of vegetation.)

Lambley

Running now in a cutting, the route approached the spectacular Lambley viaduct - the most important engineering feature between Haltwhistle and Alston. As mentioned in Chapter One, this impressive structure had nine 58 ft spans, together with seven 20 ft openings. There were also two, much smaller, 12 ft arches, the total number of openings being 18; the viaduct was built to a symmetrical design, the 58 ft spans being in the centre, while the 12 ft spans were on either side. Four 20 ft openings were situated at the north end of the bridge, and the three remaining 20 ft arches were grouped at the southern end of the viaduct. The maximum height of the bridge was about 100 ft above the River South Tyne, and there was a small footbridge beside the bases of the main piers.

The attractiveness of Lambley viaduct was enhanced by its wooded surroundings, and Alan Robinson recalled that, when he worked on the branch as a driver, 'many people would come year after year to see the magnificent viaduct' in colourful autumn. In similar vein, guard Peter Huntsman remembered that the trains would be slowed 'so that passengers could take photographs of the 100 ft high viaduct'. He recalled that, at one place, the tree tops were level with the railway, and it was possible for nature lovers to see and photograph a family of red squirrels in their natural habitat!

Lambley station was sited at the southern end of the viaduct. Situated on a sharp curve, Lambley was 4 miles 67 chains from Haltwhistle; it boasted a range of Elizabethan-style buildings with a prominent central gable. Toilet and waiting room facilities were provided in the 1890s in a single-storey wooden extension to the south of the main building, and there was a two-storey domestic block to the north. Internally, the main building contained a living room, sitting room and kitchen for the station master and his family, together with two bedrooms on the first floor. It is possible that, when first built, the building had also contained booking facilities (possibly at the north end) but for most of its life the main block was used purely for domestic purposes - indeed, there was no internal communication between the station house and the adjacent booking office.

Other features of interest at Lambley included the usual NER-style hip-roofed signal cabin, together with a small goods shed and loading dock that was (unusually) sited beside the main running line. There was, in addition, a small wooden shed between the signal box and station building which may have been the original waiting room; plans reveal that this somewhat ramshackle structure was used as a 'warehouse'.

The view from the platform at Lambley was impressive, with Lambley viaduct dominating the scene in the foreground and the unspoiled river flowing and bubbling far below. Northwards, the connecting line to Midgeholme and Brampton Junction could clearly be seen; this residual link

A panoramic view of Lambley station and viaduct showing a class 'J39' 0-6-0 at the head of the local Alston service. Note the coal wagons on the colliery branch.
N.E. Stead

The colliery sidings at Lambley, seen from a passing train on the main line. This goods-only line provided a useful connection to the Earl of Carlisle's Brampton Railway: note the NER-style interlaced turnout. *P.B. Booth*

A view from the track of the station buildings at Lambley station with its mixture of wooden and brick construction. The two-level platform again can be clearly seen.

N.E. Stead

Lambley station, seen here from the north. Note the curious, cottage-like extension on the right hand side of the main block: this was part of the station master's living accommodation, whereas the wooden extension at the far end of the building provided waiting room and booking facilities. *Lens of Sutton*

to the historic Brampton Railway remained in operation long after the rest of the system had been abandoned. The Midgeholme line — officially known as 'The Kirkhouse line' or the 'Lambley Fell branch' — was entered via a single turnout facing towards Alston, and trains from Haltwhistle had to run forward into Lambley passenger station before reversing on to the single line branch. The line immediately doubled to form a loop, and there was also a dead-end siding near the junction with the main line. Northwards, the branch continued to Harper Town, where a short siding diverged to serve a private loading dock; beyond, the line turned westwards to reach Lambley Colliery and here, a little over 1 mile from Lambley station, the branch came to an end.

There were no sidings at Lambley station, all coal and cattle traffic being handled on the Kirkhouse branch. Curiously, there was no road access to the station, and goods or passengers reached the railway by means of a rough track which left Harper Town and followed the Kirkhouse branch towards the junction; this track crossed the main line on the level and then followed the branch for several hundred yards to reach a convenient occupation bridge.

Another unusual feature of Lambley station concerned its primitve passing arrangements. There was no passing loop, as such, but one passenger and one goods train (or two goods trains) could pass if one of the trains was shunted onto the Lambley Fell branch.

Apart from its important coal and mineral traffic, Lambley also handled small amounts of other goods, including agricultural produce from the surrounding farms and general merchandise for consumption in the immediate locality. Passenger traffic was never heavy, but the station nevertheless served the needs of local inhabitants for many years; the railway was especially useful during the harsh Northumberland winters, when all other forms of transport were often halted by snow drifts.

In late Victorian days the station master was Henry Laing, who also served the community as a sub-postmaster — the local post office being at Lambley station (an unusual, but by no means unique situation in remote moorland areas). The station master around 1914 was Charles Hammond, while those employed at the station after World War II included porter-signalman Thomas Armstrong and signalwoman Hilda Thompson. Unlike Featherstone and Coanwood, Lambley retained its station master until the BR era, the usual staff complement being one station master and two porter-signalmen.

Until 1933 the single line section between Lambley and Alston had been worked on the staff-and-ticket system, but thereafter the section was worked by electric train tablet, and before proceeding beyond Lambley drivers had to hand-in their train staffs and obtain the electric tablet that permitted them to continue southwards on the final stage of their journey to Alston.

Accelerating out of Lambley station, down trains rounded a curve, and with Lambley viaduct still prominent away to the left, the line passed beneath bridge 17 — a timber occupation bridge with one central 25 ft span and two subsidiary 10 ft spans.

Climbing steadily on a succession of rising gradients, the line passed

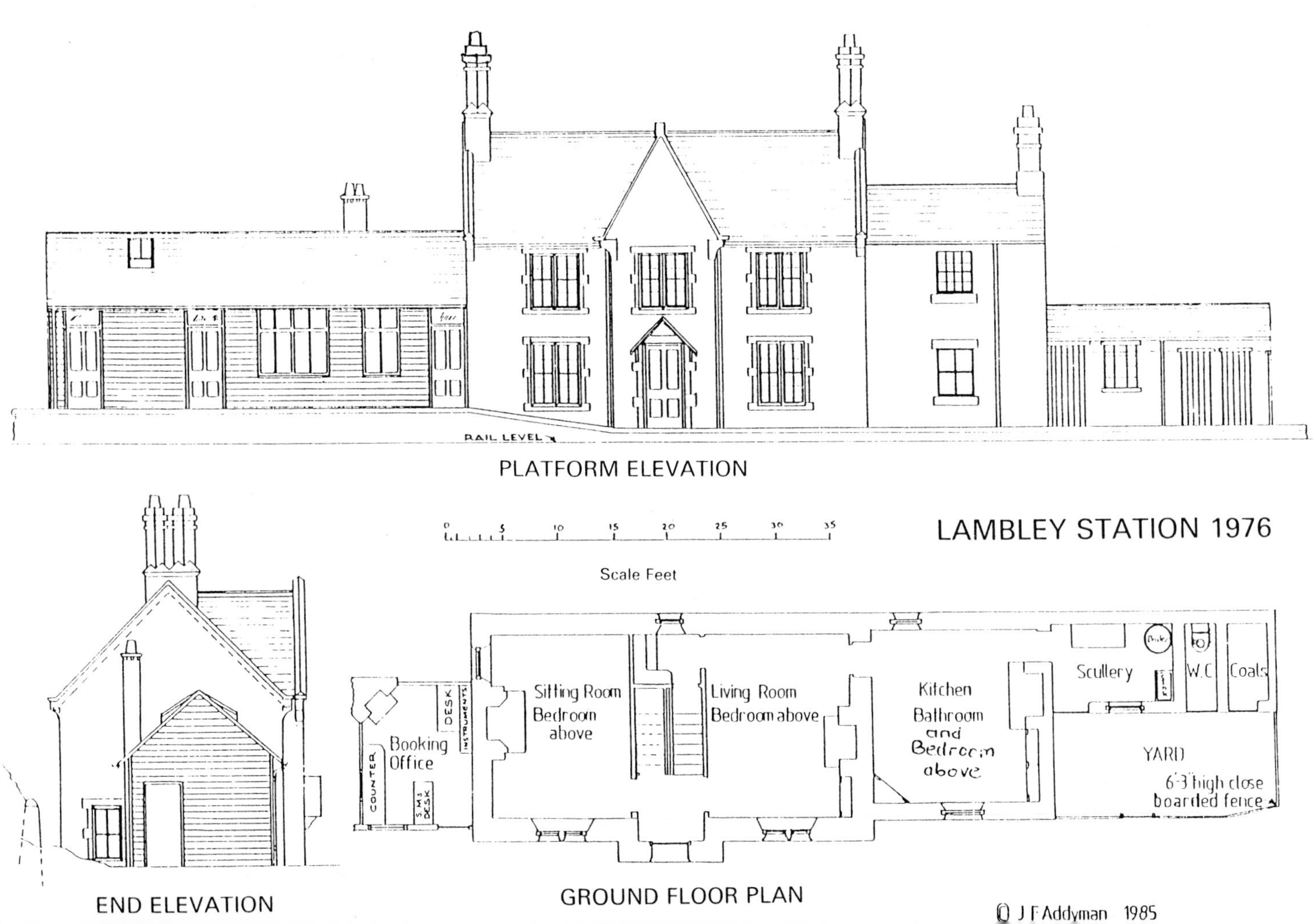
RAIL LEVEL
PLATFORM ELEVATION
LAMBLEY STATION 1976
0 5 10 15 20 25 30 35
Scale Feet
Booking Office
COUNTER
DESK
INSTRUMENTS
S.M.S DESK
Sitting Room Bedroom above
Living Room Bedroom above
Kitchen Bathroom and Bedroom above
Scullery
W.C
Coals
YARD
6'3" high close boarded fence
END ELEVATION
GROUND FLOOR PLAN
© J F Addyman 1985

through Softly Low Wood, which was followed, within a short distance, by Softly High Wood. The most impressive engineering feature on this section was Glendue Burn viaduct (bridge 21) at 5 miles 67 chains; the viaduct had five arches, each with a span of 20 ft. The highest arch was about 51 ft above water-level, and (unlike the South Tyne viaduct at Lambley) Glendue Burn viaduct was wide enough to accommodate a double track, the distance between parapets being 23 ft.

Glendue itself was a well-known beauty spot, and appreciative visitors were able to walk through this dark rocky glen to see the waterfalls in Glendue Wood. The name 'Glendue' was probably an Anglicised form of the Gaelic Glen *Dhu* (dark glen or ravine), a name which aptly described the romantic glen and its swirling, leaping moorland stream.

Bridge 24 (6 miles 54 chains) was a stone occupation bridge carrying a private road to Softley Farm over the line. The farm was situated within yards of the railway, and indeed, some of the original farm buildings were demolished when the branch was built during the 1850s. Softley Farm had been the home of the Moone family for many generations, and family tradition recalled several incidents relating to the railway. Some of these tales were recounted by the present Mrs Moone. Her husband's grandfather had been living at Softley Farm when the railway was built, and a tale handed down from father to son suggested that the cutting to the south of the farm was excavated by a contractor called Barney, who went bankrupt when he ran into unexpectedly hard rock. The works were completed by a new contractor, but the cutting was nevertheless known locally as 'Barney's Bank' in recognition of the first contractor; Mrs Moone also remembered that several houses in the vicinity were said to have been built by stone masons employed on the line in the 1850s. Another family tradition recalled how, in the 1880s, Mr Moone's grandfather had a dog called 'Hell', who was trained to wait by the railway line to collect the newspapers which were thrown onto the embankment as the train went past!

In 1947, the cutting near Softley Farm was the scene of the deep snow drift mentioned in Chapter Two, and Mrs Moone remembered that some unfortunate passengers had to spend the night on a stranded train. Roads were of course impassable, and for this reason milk from Softley was taken to the station on a horse-drawn sledge. Softley Farm was an unofficial 'stop', and it was not unknown for regular travellers to alight at this point (neighbouring Whitwham Farm was another unofficial stopping place, along with Burnstones bridge, to the south of Softley).

Southwards, the route continued its ascent at 1 in 100, easing, near the 7 mile post, to 1 in 254 and then falling slightly at 1 in 122 towards the Thinhope Burn. The railway was carried across the burn on a stone viaduct with six arches (bridge 26) five of which had skew spans of 30 ft while the sixth (over a public road) had a skew span of 39 ft. The bridge was officially known as Thinhope Burn viaduct, but local nomenclature also dubbed it 'Burnstones Bridge' because it was near the hamlet of Burnstones. Amusingly, the asymmetric design of this 37 ft high viaduct was said to have been suggested by a tramp or gypsy who happened to be passing through Burnstones when the railway builders were about to start work on the bridge! This picturesque tale is probably untrue, but the fact remains that Thinhope Burn viaduct was an unusual structure, its single road span being almost at right angles to the skew arches over the burn.

Slaggyford

Resuming its climb, the line passed under another minor road at bridge 28 (7 miles 48 chains). To the left, it was possible to catch fleeting glimpses of the village of Knaresdale. Knaresdale church was a 19th century structure of little intrinsic interest to the casual visitor (though the church yard contained the epitaph of Robert Baxter — murdered on 4th October, 1796 by a man he 'knew full well'). Of greater interest, perhaps, was a nearby farmstead built on the site of Knaresdale Hall, and once thought to be haunted. Legend had it that the Laird of Knaresdale married a young woman, who inevitably fell deeply in love with her husband's nephew. The young man's sister found out about this illicit love affair, and fearing that she would tell her uncle, the guilty pair threw the blameless girl into the moat. Later, the Laird was awakened from sleep by the ghostly apparition of his drowned niece, while his wife subsequently died of a mysterious illness; overcome with guilt, the young man threw himself into the moat, and the grim tragedy of Knaresdale Hall was thereby brought to a somewhat predictable conclusion. (Some versions of the story suggest that he simply vanished on the moors.)

Passing beneath two more bridges, the railway continued its climb towards Alston on a 1 in 122 adverse gradient. Entering some further cuttings, the route turned onto a south-easterly heading before emerging on another embankment which led, in turn, to the Knar Burn viaduct (bridge 31). Situated at 8 miles 21 chains, Knar Burn viaduct was similar to the neighbouring Glendue Burn and Thinhope Burn viaducts; it had four 30 ft stone arches, the height from water to rail level being 47 ft 9 in.

Entering a cutting that was spanned, at 8 miles 33 chains, by a stone-arched occupation bridge, trains soon reached Slaggyford (8 miles 50 chains), the penultimate stopping place between Haltwhistle and Alston.

Slaggyford was, in many ways, the most attractive station on the branch. Situated some 8 miles 49 chains from Haltwhistle, its single platform was shielded by a verdant screen of trees and shrubs which provided at least some protection from winter wind and rain. The track layout incorporated a 726 ft loop and a 270 ft dead end siding, the latter being on the down side while the platform was on the up side of the line. The siding ended on some typical NER-style coal drops, which were similar to those found elsewhere on the branch. Although Slaggyford was once a block post, early photographs suggest that the loop was not signalled for conventional passing purposes, and the presence of a small loading dock and goods store beside the line indicate that the loop was intended for use as a goods siding rather than a passing facility.

Slaggyford's passenger platform was approximately 250 ft long, and its booking office and waiting rooms were accommodated in a simple timber-framed building dating from 1890, with a slated roof and weather-boarded

The Knar Burn (or Barnesford) viaduct was situated at the 8 mile 21 chains. It had 4 spans and rose to a maximum height of 47 ft 9 in. above water level. *Ruby Makepeace*

Slaggyford station, looking north, with the running line on the left and the Anthracite Coal & Lime Co.'s siding on the right. *K. Hoole Collection*

Slaggyford, looking north towards Haltwhistle in the 1920s; the brickwork on the signal cabin (built *c.*1904) still shows signs of newness. The siding visible on the extreme right gave access to the Anthracite Coal & Lime Company's private siding.
Ruby Makepeace

A platform scene at Slaggyford, seen from a stationary freight train; the wooden building was of NER vintage. *J.W. Armstrong*

walls. The booking office occupied the south end of the structure, while the waiting room was housed in the centre of the building; a ladies' room was sited at the northernmost extremity of the wooden station building. Each of these rooms was heated by coal fires, a double-flued chimney stack being provided for the waiting and ladies' rooms while a single brick flue extended from the rear wall of the booking office. External doors gave access to the booking office and waiting rooms, but there were no doors or windows in the rear wall.

Other buildings at Slaggyford included an original Newcastle & Carlisle Railway station master's dwelling house on the down side of the line, and a brick-built North Eastern Railway signal box on the up side. There was a weigh-house in the tiny goods yard, and a platelayers' hut stood beside the line at the Alston end of the station. The goods store was situated beside the station master's house, and a tumble-down wooden shack (officially described as a 'coal house') was sited near the level crossing which bisected the station at the southern end of the platform. The crossing gates were worked by a wheel in the adjacent signal cabin — a similar arrangement being in force at the other branch stations.

The basic track layout remained unchanged for many years, the only significant alteration being the addition of a private siding to serve the Anthracite Coal & Lime Company. This new facility was installed around 1916, and it ran beside the main line for a considerable distance before terminating beside the coal company's loading dock. Entry to the dead-end siding was controlled from a ground frame which worked in conjunction with the train staff, and the line ended beneath an overhead gantry, by means of which wagons could be filled by gravity.

Once considered important enough to have its own station master, Slaggyford was later downgraded to such an extent that it could be worked by two porter-signalmen who operated the level crossing and undertook all station work. One of the last station masters had been Thomas Bell, who had worked at Slaggyford during the late Edwardian period; an earlier station master was Thomas Amos, who supervised the station during the 1880s.

Interestingly, Thomas Bell was a keen amateur historian who took a deep interest in the many stories and legends associated with Alston and the surrounding area, and he eventually put this knowledge to good use by writing an informative guidebook about South Tynedale. His literary activities did not pass unnoticed, and in December 1911 *The North Eastern Railway Magazine* printed the following note under the heading 'A NER Stationmaster's Guide Book':

> It is pleasing to know that out of the multitude of guide-books which treat of the various holiday resorts in the North of England, one at least is the work of a NER stationmaster. It possesses the explanatory title of *Handbook of Slaggyford & the South Tynedale District*, its author being Mr T. Bell, the Slaggyford Stationmaster, and it describes the wild attractiveness of the locality of which it treats in a fashion at once fresh and invigorating. Slaggyford is situate on a branch which leaves the Newcastle and Carlisle line at Haltwhistle and winds its way among hills and moorland to Alston, 'the highest market town in England'.
>
> The guide briefly sketches the story of this district from the time when Romans

made it their temporary abiding place and 'wolves were numerous in the craggy mountains'.

Mr Bell, who in a preface gratefully acknowledges the assistance of many of the best authorities in the North of England, refers interestingly to the many relics of antiquity to be found in the district, and mentions the almost pure Saxon dialect of the natives, relating a few racy anecdotes of a bygone generation. The folklore of the neighbourhood is also touched upon, its show places described and chapters are devoted even to its geology and climate. The practical uses of the guide-book are not, however, over-looked, and some 12 walks, 'mountain climbs' and 'fell-side rambles' are described with a commendable regard for detail.

Finally, the booklet — which is sold at 6*d*. — contains half a dozen fine full page illustrations, some of which must be quite a revelation to those previously unacquainted with the charms of this somewhate remote portion of our system.

In common with other railways the Alston branch served the public in perfect safety for many years, but minor accidents were not unknown, and one such incident occurred at Slaggyford during the British Railways period when an experienced driver with an otherwise spotless record ran his train through the level crossing gates. Sadly, the driver in question was approaching retirement, and although nobody was injured, the accident was a most distressing experience for a conscientious railwayman near the end of his working life.

Departing from Slaggyford, southbound trains crossed over yet another arched viaduct, with two stone spans, each of approximately 25 ft. This spanned nothing more than a farm track, and the height to rail level was just 13 ft. Like most of the other bridges between Haltwhistle and Alston, the viaduct was built to take a double track, and when the Anthracite Coal & Lime Company's private siding was laid alongside the main line, there was ample room for two lines of rails across the 23 ft wide bridge.

Climbing at 1 in 155, the single line ran first in cuttings and then on embankments as the veteran ex-NER locomotive laboured towards its destination. Over and underbridges followed one another in rapid succession as the railway crossed a series of moorland streams and farmers' tracks. To the right, travellers gazed forth upon a typical upland landscape that seemed, at first glance, to be entirely pastoral; on closer examination, however, observant travellers may have noticed a multiplicity of bumps and declivities which — to the landscape historian — indicated the presence of long-abandoned quarries and coal workings.

Running through the most spectacular part of their route, trains followed the South Tyne as it meandered south-east towards Alston. Nearby, the ancient trackway known as the 'Maiden Way' pursued a similar course between the bleak fells; thought to be of Roman origin, the Maiden Way was later incorporated into the Pennine Way long-distance footpath.

Passing under bridge 39 (9 miles 42 chains) the line approached Thornhope Burn and here, at 9 miles 56 chains, the railway-builders had been faced with a considerable engineering problem. The solution was another large and expensive arched stone viaduct; the Thornhope Burn viaduct (bridge 40) had four 30 ft spans, and its maximum height was 45 ft above local ground level. Confusingly, the bridge was known locally as Lintley Burn viaduct, although NER sources suggest that 'Thornhope Burn' was the official name.

Barhaugh Colliery Sidings

From Thornhope Burn viaduct the route continued towards the site of Barhaugh Colliery Sidings (9 miles 62 chains). Situated on the down side, the sidings faced Haltwhistle and were controlled from a 2-lever ground frame; a single turnout gave access to the running line, and the siding immediately doubled to form a run-round loop. Safety points prevented breakaways from entering the main line, and two short spurs extended from the loop to end in buffer stops. Barhaugh Pit was sited at some distance from the sidings, but an aerial ropeway enabled coal to be rapidly transported to the waiting railway wagons.

Board of Trade records reveal that the 'siding connection for Barhaugh Colliery' was inspected by Colonol von Donop on 2nd April, 1913, and the BoT Inspector's brief report may be worth quoting insofar as it contains a few further details of this little-recorded industrial siding:

> Sir,
>
> I have the honour to report for the information of the Board of Trade that in compliance with the instructions contained in your minute . . . I have inspected the new works near Slaggyford, on the Alston branch of the North Eastern Railway.
>
> On the down side . . . a new connection, which is facing to down trains and which leads to sidings, has been laid in on the single line. The points and signals are worked from a ground frame of 2 levers, which is locked by the staff of the section.
>
> Owing to the gradient on which the new connection is situated, it will be necessary for traffic to and from the siding to be worked with the engine at the lower end of the train, and this the Company undertakes to carry out.
>
> The interlocking is correct . . . so, subject to the above mentioned undertaking, I can recommend the Board of Trade to sanction the new works being brought into use.

It should perhaps be pointed out that Barhaugh (or 'Blackcleugh') pit was a very small colliery. It was opened in 1909, and 14 men were at work there by 1925. The labour force had dropped to just 5 by 1930, and although 'The Barhaugh Anthracite & Limestone Co's Siding' was still listed in the 1938 *Railway Clearing House Handbook of Stations*, the colliery had apparently fallen into disuse by the start of World War II.

Continuing south-eastwards, the line reached the steepest part of its route, and, with the sharp exhaust beats of the labouring engine leaving no doubt that the general direction was now upwards, trains tackled the fearsome 1 in 56 rising gradient between Barhaugh Sidings and Dyke House Farm; the 1 in 56 climb commenced near the 9¾ mile post and extended for one mile to the 10¾ mile post. Bridges on this section included an arched stone occupation bridge at 10 miles 26 chains, an underline occupation bridge at 10 miles 48 chains, two small underline culverts, and another stone occupation bridge at 10 miles 63 chains.

With the gradients easing to 1 in 176 (after a brief descent) trains crossed the triple-arched Lortburn or Whitley Burn viaduct (bridge 48), which carried them some 34 ft above the tiny Lort Burn. To the right, a Roman fort known as Whitley Castle occupied an elevated position above the 1,000 ft contour line, while abandoned lead mines, coal pits and stone quarries occupied even higher positions above 1,200 ft. Still maintaining its south-easterly heading, the railway climbed towards Alston at 1 in 176, with the South Tyne still visible to the east and two thousand foot fells towering high above the line.

As the trains crossed Lortburn viaduct travellers could, by glancing to the left, see the little church at Kirkhaugh; nestling in beautiful, wooded surroundings, the church was rebuilt in the 1860s to plans drawn-up by the then Vicar, the Reverend Octavius James. The remodelled church featured a curiously-slender spire that was said to have been copied from an example in the Black Forest, and for this reason Kirkhaugh Church was sometimes referred to as 'The German Church'. Former BR guard George Kipling regarded the church as a familiar landmark on his daily journeys up and down the branch, and he visited it on several occasions to 'have a little tune on the organ'.

Onwards, the railway was carried along an embankment, and with Kirkside Wood visible on the far side of the South Tyne, trains passed over two more occupation bridges in quick succession. Beyond, the line crossed Gilderdale Burn on a triple-arched stone viaduct at 11 miles 48 chains (bridge 51).

The Gilderdale viaduct was the ninth major bridge encountered since leaving Haltwhistle; it had three unequal spans, the largest of which had a width of 49ft 2in. while the two flanking arches had smaller spans of 29ft 6in. The viaduct was 21 ft wide between parapets (i.e. wide enough to take a double track) and it rose 34 ft above the Gilderdale Burn. This viaduct was the scene of the March 1948 derailment, which occurred after the harsh winter of that year. The train involved in this incident was thrown completly off the track, one coach being tipped onto its side while the other vehicles remained upright; the locomotive — an 0–6–0 running tender first — was also derailed, though its tender stayed on the track.

LAMBLEY VIADUCT

Chapter Four

Along the Line; Alston

The Gilderdale Burn marked the boundary between the counties of Northumberland and Cumberland, and having crossed the burn, trains undulated through a pastoral Cumbrian landscape on a series of favourable gradients. Approaching Alston, the line soared across the tenth and last viaduct - another triple-arched structure with a central span of 39 ft and two subsidiary spans of 39 ft 6in. With four long stone sidings now visible to the left, branch trains finally entered Alston station and here, some 13 miles 14 chains from Haltwhistle, the scenic journey along the South Tyne Valley came to an end.

The terminus was an interesting, mid-Victorian station replete with a variety of unusual and original features. The single line came to an end beside a 318 ft platform, with a run-round loop to the west and a 42 ft diameter turntable at the very end of the line. The platform line was flanked by a short carriage siding which stopped just short of the turntable, and there was a small, stone-built engine shed beside the passenger station; this was served by a direct connection to the turntable - enabling incoming locomotives to retire to the shed after uncoupling and drawing forward for turning.

The Passenger Station

The main station buildings were on the down (i.e. east) side of the line, and they were built in the Elizabethan-style with mullioned windows, tall chimneys and decorative gables. The single platform was protected by an overall roof which rested upon a buttressed wall on one side, and the station building on the other. The engine shed, with its workshop and water tower, was joined to the train shed, and there was, as a result, an interesting range of architecturally-similar structures grouped together at the end of the line. All were built of semi-irregular stonework which was laid, for the most part, in horizontal courses with occasional patches of 'snecked' masonry. The main station building was, in later years at least, covered with cement (or similar) rendering on its three most-exposed sides (one wonders if the station master's accommodation was susceptible to damp?)

These distinctive Newcastle & Carlisle buildings remained more or less unchanged for many years, and apart from the rebuilding of the train shed (referred to in Chapter Two) the most significant alterations took place in 1904-5, when the North Eastern Railway carried out a programme of improvements designed to increase passenger amenities. A single-storey extension was added to the northern end of the original building, and at the same time the booking office was adapted to provide additional parcels accommodation. The new extension block contained a variety of new facilities including (from north to south) a store, a boiler house, a new porters' room and a new gentlemen's toilet. The main block remained more or less unaltered during the 1904-5 upheavals, and the ground floor of this two-storey building continued to provide booking office, waiting room and parcels facilities. The first floor, meanwhile, was used as domestic

Alston station photographed in March 1954, showing a class 'J39', No. 64858 standing under the overall roof having just arrived from Haltwhistle on a local service. The smokebox plate number is 53A, with the word 'DAIRYCOATES' on the buffer beam.
Ian L. Wright

A panoramic view of Alston station and yard seen from just above the gasworks at the turn of the century (note the old signal box which was replaced in 1905). A goods train is being shunted in the yard with a spare engine in attendance. The River South Tyne can be seen in the background.
Lens of Sutton

accommodation for the station master and his family, and one end of the lower floor was also used as living accommodation; a new scullery was added to the southern end of the main block in 1904.

Passengers entered the station building by means of a passageway at the north end of the building — though prior to 1905 they had walked straight into the booking office through a door which was afterwards used as a parcels lobby. A further entrance at the south end of the building opened into the station master's private entrance lobby, while the platform façade had separate doors for the booking office, waiting room and ladies' room.

Unusually, the southern end of the passenger platform terminated in a flight of stone steps instead of the customary sloping ramp — which was in a sense illegal under normal Board of Trade regulations (although the fact that this end of the platform was not used by departing trains presumably meant that a conventional ramp was unnecessary). The platform itself was constructed of rubble and other infilling material, its central core being held in place by a solid, snecked stone face. The top surface was paved with stone slabs, but unusually, the platform edge was more or less flush with the stone facing, and although a small lip or overhang was discernible, the prominent 'pediment' feature seen on most railway platforms was absent. There was, however, a slightly more pronounced overhang on the section of platform beneath the train shed, and this section was also built of coursed stonework instead of the random blocks used along the remainder of the platform. (Such minor changes in structure and materials indicate that the platform had been extended and raised at various times in its long life!)*

The Goods Department

Alston's track layout was relatively complex, and in addition to its run-round and locomotive facilities this Pennine branch terminus had extensive goods sidings, with a hip-roofed goods shed and some characteristic North Eastern Railway coal drops; one of the yard sidings extended southwards and passed beneath the Hexham road to terminate in a privately-owned stone yard. Other facilities included the usual loading docks, cattle pens, and a 4 ton yard crane.

It was noticeable, even to the casual observer, that the goods yard had been laid out with ore traffic in mind, and to facilitate the efficient transfer of stone and other minerals between road vehicles and waiting railway wagons the level of the yard had been built-up to about 4½ ft above rail level — enabling minerals to be transhipped from what was, in effect, a vast loading dock. This raised loading area was flanked by two goods sidings, one of which (near the passenger station) had a length of 116 yards while the other was 150 yards long; these two sidings could accommodate 16 and 21 short-wheelbase wagons respectively.

The coal drops were served by two more sidings, each with a length of 139 yards, and the goods shed spanned a fifth siding, the length of which was 90 yards. Another lengthy goods siding ran along the eastern edge of the yard, while the siding beneath the Hexham road increased the station's already ample capacity by a further 30 wagons.

* At one time, from 12″ to 2′6″.

A glimpse of the rarely-photographed down sidings at Alston. Used for stone traffic, these parallel sidings also formed a useful storage facility. *P.B. Booth*

A view north towards the down sidings at Alston, with the South Tyne visible to the left and an NER-type 'sleepered lead' in the foreground. *H.C. Casserley*

Class 'G5', 0–4–4T No. 67315 pauses in front of Alston signal box during a spell of shunting in the 1950s. The slotted-post shunting signal is worthy of note as is the Alston branch snow-plough. *J.W. Armstrong*

Alston station on 24th August, 1954, looking south towards the passenger station. Items of interest include the slotted post signals, the small 'Alston' nameplate on the side of the signal box and the low retaining wall which delineated the western edge of the station site. *R.F. Roberts*

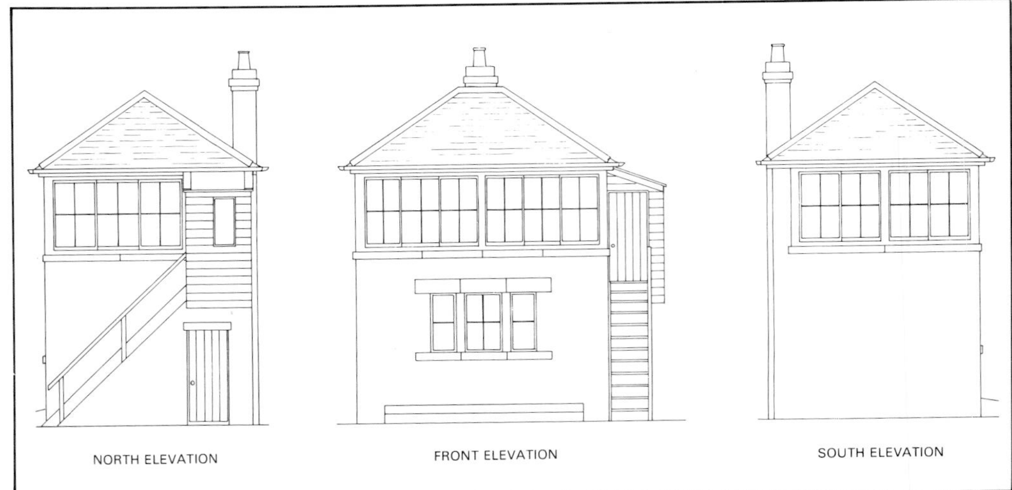

Alston station signal box. *Drawing courtesy John Addyman*

Another view of the north-end of Alston station and engine shed, showing the adjoining train shed and passenger platform. The small coaling stage can be seen to advantage in this 1956 photograph. *P.B. Booth*

Alston goods shed from the north showing the siding which extended beneath the Hexham road to reach a private stoneyard; this was in later years used mainly as a storage siding.
P.B. Booth

Alston goods shed on 21st May, 1956. The wooden weigh-bridge hut can be seen to the right. The lean-to goods office was a later addition to the hip-roofed goods shed.
P.B. Booth

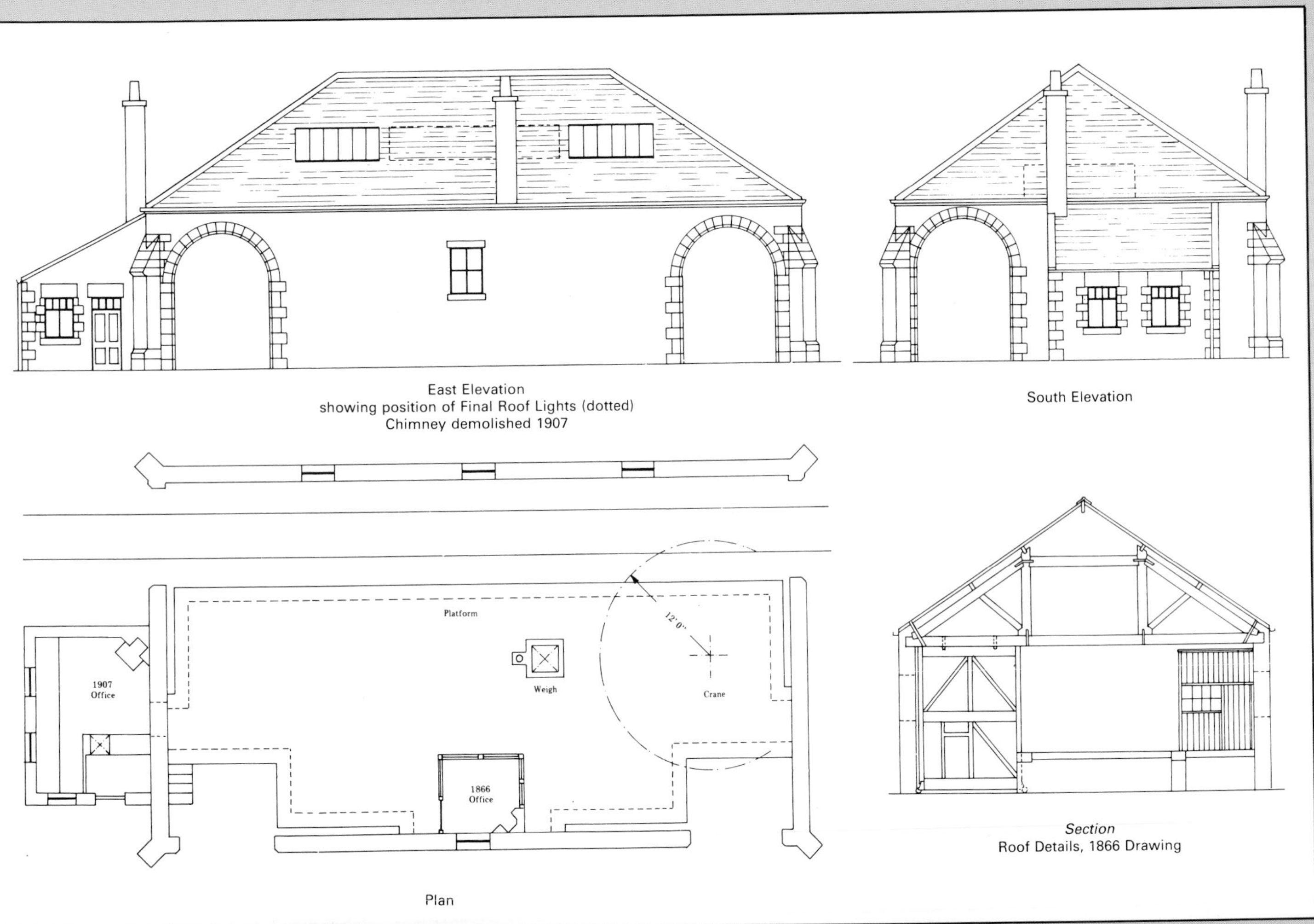

East Elevation
showing position of Final Roof Lights (dotted)
Chimney demolished 1907

South Elevation

Plan

Section
Roof Details, 1866 Drawing

A detailed view of the northern end of Alston engine shed; the building to the right was fitted-out as a mess room and workshop. The swan-necked water crane can be clearly seen. *P.B. Booth*

A useful view of Alston's NER style coal drops, which originally provided sixteen, 12.25 ton cells (though one was later converted into a small storage shed). *P.B. Booth*

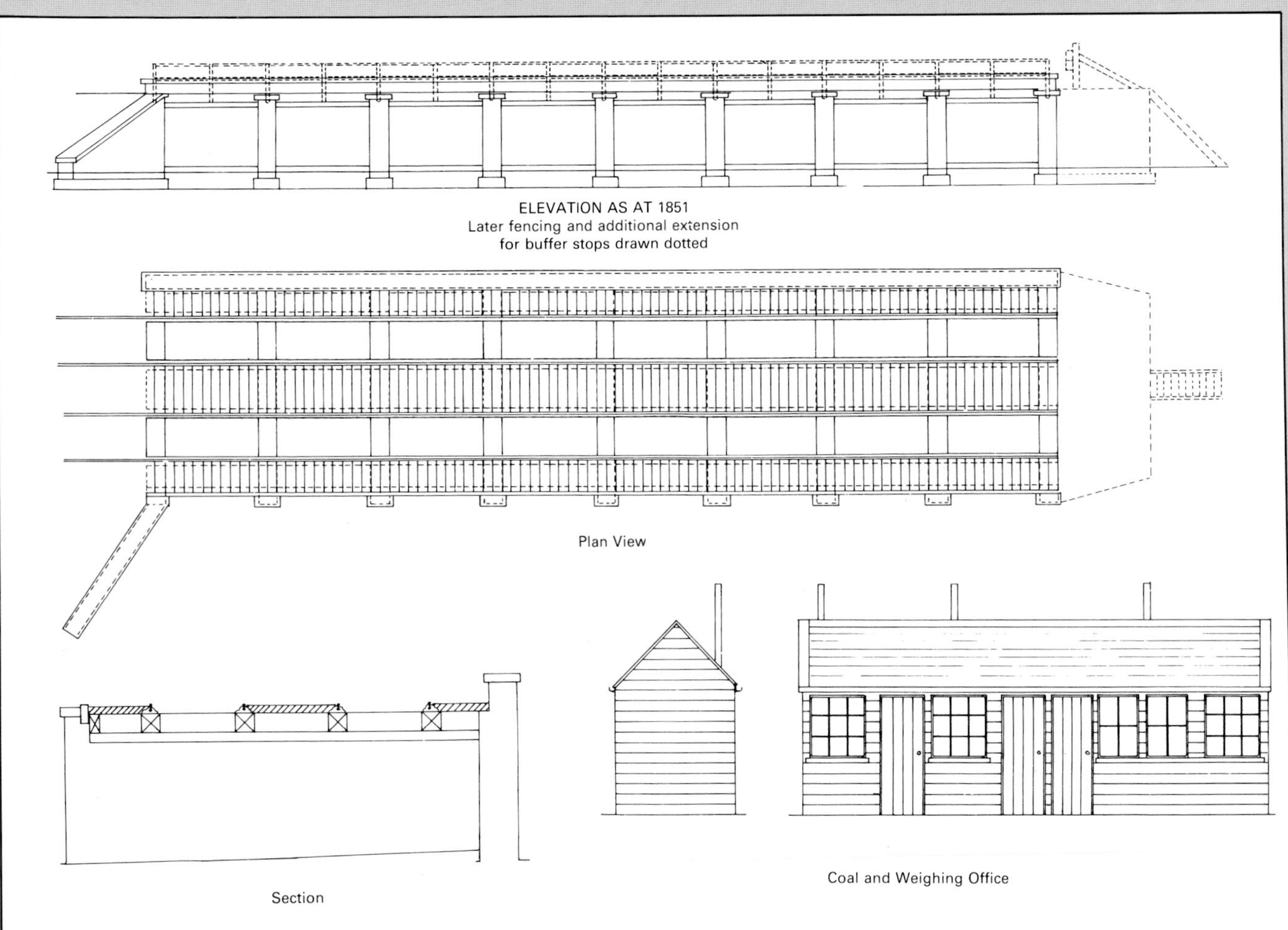
ELEVATION AS AT 1851
Later fencing and additional extension
for buffer stops drawn dotted
Plan View
Section
Coal and Weighing Office

In total, the goods yard was able to accommodate up to 152 wagons, while the four stone sidings at the northern end of the station could hold a further 150 short wheelbase goods vehicles — making Alston's total freight handling capacity some 300 wagons at any one time.

The above-mentioned stone sidings (sometimes referred to as the 'down sidings') were used by local mineral firms such as the Alston & Nentforce Quarry Company and the Belgian-owned Vielle Montagne Zinc Company. They were copiously-equipped with loading banks and gantries for handling stone, ore and other minerals, and in addition to limestone which came by road, these sidings were once served by an aerial flight and a 2 ft gauge tramway; the aerial flight conveyed ore from nearby Blagill Quarry, while the tramway brought limestone down from Newshield Quarry (both worked by the Alston Lime & Coal Company). Mineral traffic remained an important element in Alston branch operation until the 1960s — one of the last sources of regular traffic being bags of fluorspar from the Anglo-Austral mines at Nenthead.

Another source of goods traffic during the British Railways period was metal castings made by Precision Products (Cumberland) Ltd. This company had been formed in 1947 to exploit a new casting system known as the Shaw process. Developed in Newcastle, the Shaw process was a split mould system that could easily be adapted for the production of small steel castings — as such it was ideal for use in the production of golf club heads, and after 1957 Precision Products despatched large numbers of these items by rail from Alston.

Coal was, of course, a major source of inwards freight traffic, and several different coal merchants used the goods yard at various times. These included John Place, Malcolm Graham and Arthur Wright; Mr Place used a horse drawn vehicle for delivery purposes, while Mr Graham was a farmer as well as a local coal merchant. Additionally, NER station masters were also permitted to act as coal agents, and it appears that this practice continued at Alston until recent years.

Much of the coal brought into Alston by rail was burned in domestic hearths, but there were one or two small industrial users – notably the Alston Foundry and the small gas works on the other side of the Hexham road. Prior to nationalisation, this tiny gas-producing plant had been owned by the Hexham Gas Light & Coke Company; the works was situated within yards of the privately-owned stone yard mentioned above, but incoming coal was usually moved into the gas company's yard by horse and cart. The adjacent stone siding was, on the other hand, occasionally used by the gas company to load 40 gallon tar barrels, which could be rolled along a short trackway to the waiting railway wagons. This practice had of course ceased by the British Railways period, and in the 1950s the former stone siding (once used by the Alston Lime Company) was treated primarily as a storage siding.

The main building in Alston goods yard was the goods shed. This stone-built structure measured approximately 70 ft × 40 ft at ground level. Large arched entrances enabled road vehicles to back-up to the internal loading platform, and similar apertures spanned the single rail line that passed

Station Buildings at Alston

A view of the rear of Alston station building, photographed in 1956; the snow plough alongside the signal box is visible in the background. *P.B. Booth*

The 4 ton hand yard crane, and the rear of the station buildings are all clearly visible in this October 1963 view, with a Bedford 26 seat OB coach awaiting its passengers. *Oakwood Collection*

These two views taken in July 1956 show in close-up the end of the line at Alston after the removal of the turntable and subsequent extension of the running line across the former turntable pit; note the absence of a platform ramp. *P.B. Booth*

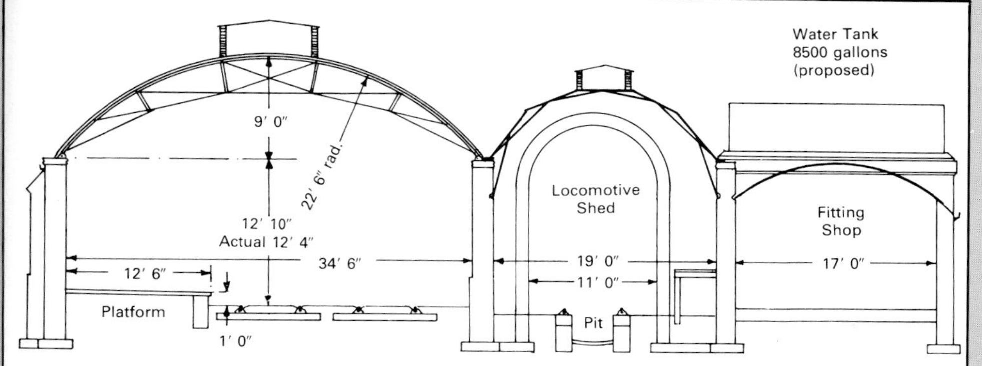

Section of Station Buildings
(Platform, Locomotive shed, Fitting shop, 1852)

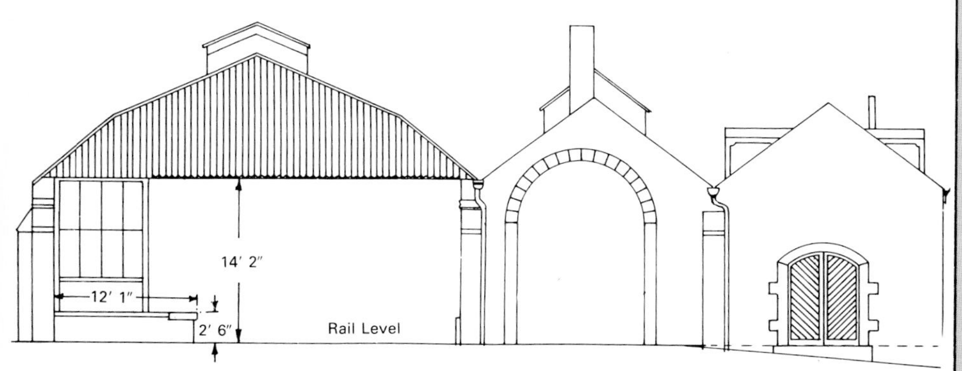

End elevation as at demolition

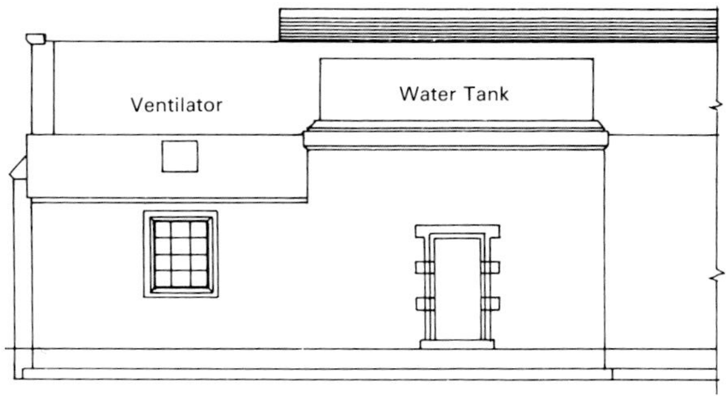

Fitting shop and stores (elevation of 1852)

The station buildings at Alston; the lean-to building was a later addition.
Ken Hoole Collection

Milepost number 13 (from Haltwhistle) seen here on the down side of the approach to Alston station. The 'dolly' signal (raised) is worthy of note. This controlled the access to the main running line from the goods yards.
Ken Hoole Collection

2374 CHILD

2nd-SINGLE

Haltwhistle To

FEATHERSTONE PARK

(N) Fare 0/4

FOR CONDITIONS SEE OVER

CHILD 2374

No. 64812, class 'J39' (shed 52C) seen here at Alston with a special. Note the outer track being used as a coach siding. *N.E. Stead Collection*

With No. 64812 in the locomotive shed and No. 67315 standing in the station; making this a busy scene at Alston, on a rainy day. *N.E. Stead Collection*

A rare glimpse of the somewhat dark interior of Alston station platform.
N.E. Stead Collection

through the shed. Internally, the shed contained a fixed hand crane, and from 1907 there was a small goods office at the southern end of the main structure.

Other buildings in the goods yard included a sleeper-built stable and a wooden weighbridge office; the stable was a lean-to structure abutting the north end of the goods shed, while the weighbridge office stood at the southern end of the goods yard near the main entrance gates. The latter building was a timber-framed shed clad in horizontal weather boarding with a slated roof - it also contained office accommodation for the local coal merchants.

Other Details

An interesting feature of Alston station and goods yard were its interlaced turnouts or - to use their local name - 'sleepered leads'. Such turnouts made use of ordinary sleepers in lieu of the extra-long timbers normally employed in pointwork, and they were at one time common throughout the former NER system.

The terminus was fully signalled, and, even in the post-war era, railway archaeologists could have found genuine ex-NER slotted post semaphores, complete with their stylish, McKenzie & Holland pattern finials; the bracketed down home was a particularly long-lived example - though sadly, this NER veteran had lost its distinctive 4 ft high finial. The station was controlled from an NER, brick-built signal box standing on the up side of the line; this had replaced a timber-built original around 1904. The replacement box was a hip-roofed design which, in LNER fashion, carried 'ALSTON' nameboards on each side rather than on the main facade.

Maps indicate that there had once been a snow plough shed in the vicinity of the signal box, this building was built around 1904, but had gone by 1930 and the Alston snow plough was thereafter parked in the open. J.B. Dawson recalled that, when he first visited Alson in the 1920s, the snow plough was 'No. 4, built in 1888, which in 1938 became DE 900560'. This snow plough was scrapped in the early 1950s, and in its place BR sent one of the then-new 981-992 series; the new plough remained at Alston until the closure of Alston shed in 1959.

The LNER was the poorest of the 'Big Four' companies created as a result of the 1921 Railways Act, but this somewhat impoverished undertaking was frequently an innovator. Its advertising policies, for example, were both innovative and imaginative, while the company was the very first to introduce so-called 'camping coaches' as a means of encouraging tourist traffic.

In August 1933, *The Railway Magazine* announced that the LNER was adapting a number of old passenger vehicles for use as 'complete holiday homes . . . in sites in the dales of Northumberland, the Esk Valley, the Pennines, the Cheviots, and other favourite spots'. The coaches involved in this conversion were ten former Great Northern Railway six-wheelers, and the conversion was effected by the simple expedient of removing some of the internal partitions to form an open living room and dining area - two compartments being retained as sleeping cabins. These old vehicles were then sent to selected stations in the North Eastern area, Alston being one of the first locations.

The camping coaches were an immediate success, and they were soon attracting customers throughout the summer months. The Alston vehicle could accommodate six people, the rent (during the mid-1930s) being £2 10*s*. per week during the summer and £2 at the beginning and end of the holiday season. Towels, bed linen, cutlery and other essentials were provided by the railway company, but people staying in the coach had to use the nearby station buildings for water and toilet facilities. The kitchen area was equipped with cupboards, a sink, and two primus stoves, while the sleeping compartments were fitted with bunk beds.

It is believed that when first installed on the Alston line, the camping coach retained its ordinary teak brown livery, but the LNER's attractive green and cream 'tourist' livery was later applied to all of the company's camping coaches in an attempt to brighten-up their appearance. The coach was normally parked in a quiet position at the end of the 'down sidings', in convenient proximity to the river. The vehicle involved was probably former GNR third class coach No. 42081, which was designated 'CC4' in the LNER camping coach numbering scheme.

The Locomotive Department

The engine shed was a 'through' structure with doors at each end. Internally, it contained an inspection pit, while connecting doors gave access to an adjacent workshop with lathes, a smithy and other equipment for carrying out minor repairs to the branch engines. Part of the workshop was furnished as a mess room and store room, and a 7,000 gallon water tank was built into the roof; the shed proper was about 85 ft long, and both of its entrances had arched apertures.

Watering facilities were available from a characteristic North Eastern Railway swan-necked water crane, and there was a primitive wooden coaling stage beside the shed road. Locomotive coal was brought to Alston in loco coal wagons which were then stationed beside the coaling stage so that manual coaling could take place. Alternatively, locomotive coal could be stockpiled ready for use in a coal stack beside the engine siding.

Mr Sam Wright worked at Alston in 1920 as a relief cleaner, and he remembered that his duties included, not only cleaning, but also coaling and a range of other tasks:

> My duties were to thoroughly clean the locomotive, fill the bunker from an open coal wagon (in all weathers), obtain sand for the sand boxes and fill the tank with water for the first journey from Alston to Haltwhistle.

Mr Wright was also able to throw further light on the engine that plunged into South Tyne after running away from the engine shed. He suggested that the accident was caused by a hapless cleaner who inadvertently over-filled the boiler of 'BTP' 0–4–4T No. 60:

> It was during the movement from the engine shed to the coaling wagon that the cleaner made a very great mistake. The boiler had been over-filled, so when he opened the regulator the engine 'caught the water', and under such circumstances it is almost impossible to close the regulator — hence 'BTP' locomotive No. 60 ended up standing on her bunker in the South Tyne River.

On a footnote, it is significant that Mr Wright remembered the runaway engine ending up on its bunker; some secondary sources claim that the locomotive remained upright, but the photograph reproduced in Ken Hoole's book *North Eastern Branch Line Termini* shows noticeable damage to the bunker and cab — suggesting that the 0–4–4T did indeed land on its rear end. (It is interesting too, to find that Mr Wright's first-hand account refers to the engine being coaled and watered at the time of the accident, whereas secondary sources claim that the locomotive was unattended.)

Alston Personalities

In employment terms, Alston station was comparatively important, and in a small community which, by the turn-of-the-century, had a population of barely 3,000, its labour force of porters, signalmen, booking clerks, labourers and locomotive crews constituted a sizeable chunk of the working population. The station master, in 1894, was Joseph Walton; later, around 1900, the station master was John Railton, while in 1925 the local station master was Joseph Little.

Those employed at Alston in the Edwardian period included signal porter J. Surtees, foreman J. Armstrong, goods clerk P.E. Millican, junior clerk F. Godfrey, porter J. Dowson, goods porter J. Davidson, driver William Moore, and guard J. Brown. Many of these Alston employees subsequently worked at other North Eastern Railway stations — among them J. Surtees, who later served as a signalman at Hexham, and F. Godfrey who, after promotion, became station master at Knaresborough.

Although some men were content to remain at one station for many years, other, perhaps more ambitious employees moved from place to place in a constant search for promotion. Clerical grades were expected to apply for higher posts after serving a sort of 'apprenticeship' as juniors, and for this reason the turnover of junior clerks was surprisingly high. The pages of *The*

North Eastern Railway Magazine record the names of many of these transient staff — in 1911, for example, E. Holmes came to Alston from Usworth (near Sunderland) while in 1914 goods clerk L. Sproat left Alston to take up a new position at Heads Nook (on the Newcastle & Carlisle line near Carlisle). Another local clerk — Mr D. Walton — started his railway career at Alston in 1866 and subsequently transferred to Hexham; after further service at Brampton Junction, Carlisle, and elsewhere, he moved to Tyneside, and finally retired as chief goods clerk at Tyne Dock after 45 years service on the North Eastern Railway. Mr Walton was, in fact, a native of the Alston area, and it is amusing to relate that when in the Newcastle area he was referred to as coming from what Tynesiders called 'The West Country'!

The workforce at Alston in more recent years included goods porter Sidney Beadle, goods clerk Charlie Walton, booking clerk Ivan Edgar, permanent way men Robert Armstrong, Ned Dickinson, George Watson and Arthur Harrison, and signalman Jimmy Spottiswood. There were several female employees during and after World War II, and these included booking clerk Anne Harrison, signalwoman Mary Middleton and porteress Jenny Lowe.

Mrs Middleton worked in the signal box for about five years, and was the wife of a long-serving Alston guard — her son Arthur Middleton spent many happy hours in and around the station and later became a railwayman. He remembered many of those employed at the terminus during the early British Railways period; booking clerk Ivan Edgar, for instance, was a meticulous worker, while lengthman Arthur Harrison was another dedicated railwayman who walked the Lambley to Alston section daily to check the permanent way — Mr Middleton recalled that on a clear day one could hear him 'knocking in the wooden keys for many miles'!

The station staff during the 1950s, generally consisted of 1 station master, 2 passenger clerks, 1 goods clerk, 1 goods porter and 2 porter-signalmen, together with 2 Alston-based passenger guards and 1 goods guard. The guards employed at Alston around 1950–60 included Frank Birkett, Mr Middleton and Peter Huntsman, together with Lancaster Patterson, J. Eglin, George Kipling and R.H. Jackson. George Kipling remembered that his former colleague Lancaster Patterson was 'always very smartly dressed, and was well-liked by all of the passengers — he was very helpful to everybody'. The station master at Alston after World War II was Mr Crags, and he was followed, around 1955, by William Wood; Mr Wood remained until the early 1960s, and was then replaced by Mr Summers.

Among those employed as locomotive drivers after World War II were Tommy Stanhard, Alan Robinson, Steward Walton, and Maurice Peart; Maurice Peart enjoyed a long association with the branch (he became a butcher after closure). Others employed in the locomotive department were night fireman Frank Baker and lad cleaners Roland Emerson and Alwyn Hind. Arthur Middleton remembered Mr Baker as a very hard working and dedicated employee who started work at about 4 am to ensure that the branch engines were ready for the following day's work. Roland Emerson was another conscientious worker, but instead of following the usual BR career pattern of becoming first a fireman and then a driver he joined the

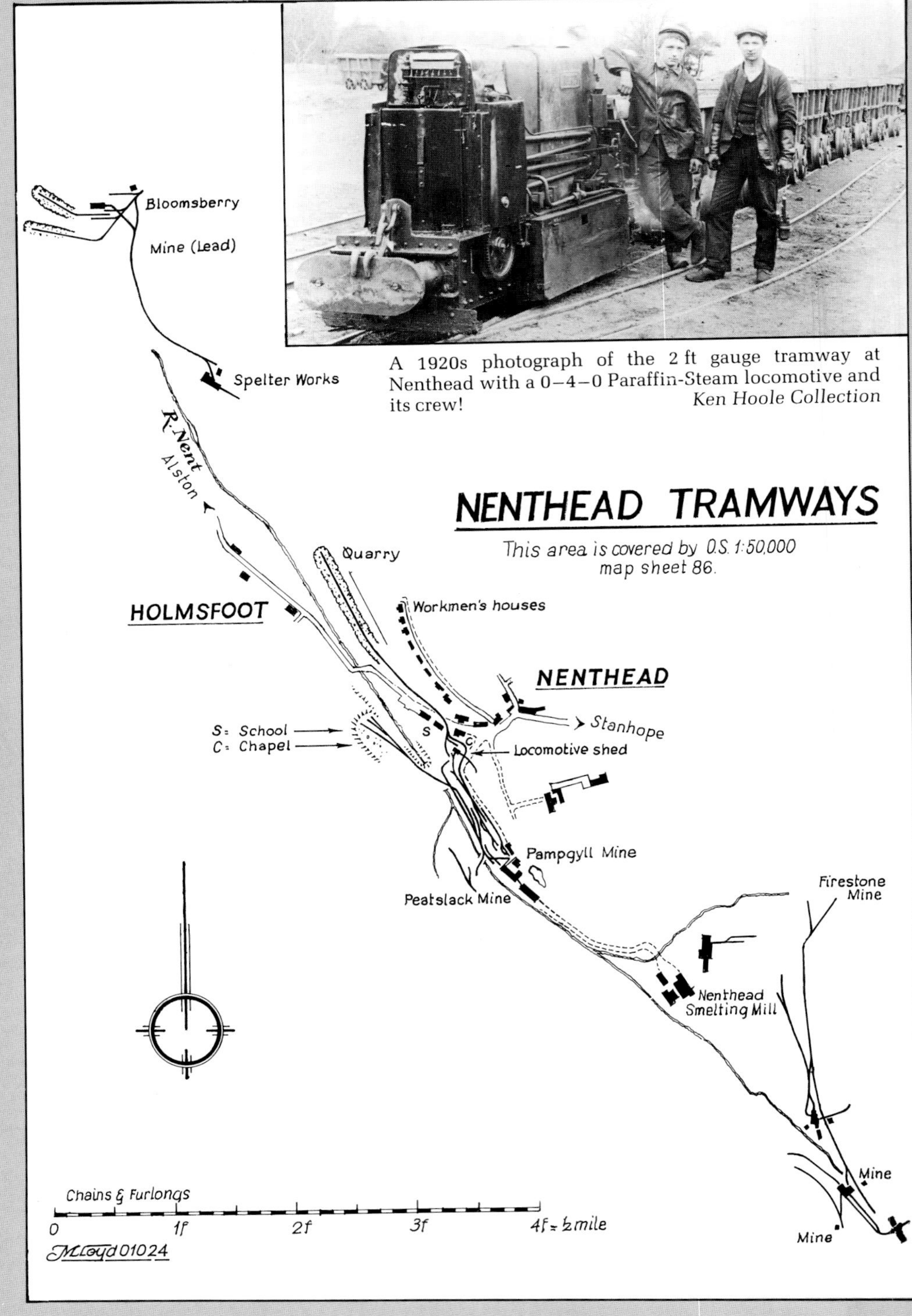

A 1920s photograph of the 2 ft gauge tramway at Nenthead with a 0–4–0 Paraffin-Steam locomotive and its crew! *Ken Hoole Collection*

armed forces. There were, in all, about a dozen people employed in the locomotive department, including 4 drivers, 4 firemen, 1 night fireman and 3 cleaners.

Alston's total staffing establishment was — taking into consideration all of those employed at the station and in the locomotive and permanent way departments — about 28, although this figure could be increased if (for example) extra staff were sent to the station for training or relief purposes. Additionally, the terminus provided employment for a varying number of coal merchants, and it would probably be true to say that, until the closure of Alston engine shed in 1959, the station employed up to 30 men and women at any one time. Thereafter, the staffing establishment at Alston was progressively reduced, and as we shall see in the following chapter, the once-flourishing terminus ultimately became little more than a halt.

Some other Points of Interest

Alston station was conveniently-sited in relation to the town, and having left their trains, passengers could easily walk the short distance from the station to the market square. There was a considerable difference in elevation between the station — which was about 920 ft above mean sea level — and the nearby Market Place, which had an elevation of 963 ft. Proceeding from market place to Townhead the visitor found himself or herself over 1,100 ft above sea level. The overwhelming impression was of a solid, stone-built town clinging grimly to the hillside, and although most of the houses were of 19th century origin the changing levels and random positioning of these grey stone buildings imparted an air of great antiquity. Many buildings were enlivened by the application of yellow or red colour-wash, and a few houses had outside staircases — a lingering relic of the days when animals occupied the ground floors! The town was, in some ways, similar to its counterparts on the Scottish side of the border, the underlying similarities being reinforced, not only by Alston's architectural traditions, but also by the character of its people.

Alston had been a lead mining centre for centuries, but there were few visible reminders of the great days of lead mining. The London Lead Company had sold their leases to the Nenthead & Tynedale Lead & Zinc Co. in 1882, and in 1896 the leases were resold to the Belgian-owned Vielle Montagne Zinc Company; finally, in 1949, the latter company sold out to Anglo-Austral Mines Ltd. Anglo-Austral's operations were modest in comparison to earlier mining ventures, and the company produced no more than about 16 tons of bagged fluorspar a day (each bag was, however, deceptively heavy, and goods porter Sidney Beadle would often complain about their weight!).

The outlying hamlet of Nenthead was the true centre of lead mining in the Alston area, and it is interesting to note that Alston was linked to its near-neighbour by a 5 mile-long underground drainage channel known as the Nent Force level. This impressive subterranean waterway was built by the Commissioners of Greenwich Hospital, and it flowed into the River Nent near Alston station. Engineered by Richard Walton and John Smeaton

(1724–92), the Nent Force Level was built over a long period between 1776 and 1842. The completed waterway was wide enough to accommodate passenger-carrying boats, and it rapidly became a popular tourist attraction. Late Victorian editions of *Kelly's Directory of Cumberland* contained the following short description:

> The Grand Aqueduct, called Nent Force Level, cut by order of the Trustees of the Hospital, extends to Nent Head, a distance of five miles underground. Several boats are kept in it, and guides are in readiness at any of the inns for those who wish to explore these subterraneous wonders. Its mouth is near the town of Alston, where the river Nent forms a very romantic waterfall.

Sadly, the entrance to Alston's underground waterway was later destroyed by modern quarrying operations, and visitors to the town after World War II were unable to find much evidence of this little-known feat of mining engineering.

In addition to the Nent Force Level, the Alston/Nenthead area contained much of interest to transport historians — notably the 2 ft gauge narrow gauge railways that formerly served the local quarries. These little-known industrial systems had their own locomotives, some of which were apparently fired by paraffin in an attempt to reduce smoke emission below ground (there are suggestions that at least one of the engines employed at Nenthead was an early internal combustion machine — former miners recall the noxious fumes emitted by this locomotive).

Before leaving Alston in order to deal with the post-nationalisation period, it is worth recalling that, if earlier plans had come to fruition, the branch would have extended beyond its original terminus to reach Middleton-in-Teesdale, from where the Tees Valley Railway would have formed a convenient outlet to the south and east. Plans for such a line were first mooted in the 1860s, but the Tees Valley line, when opened in 1868, ended at Middleton-in-Teesdale. The scheme was revived in 1873 when a group of entrepreneurs deposited plans for a 'Cumberland & Cleveland Junction Railway' between Alston and Middleton-on-Teesdale. This ambitious project fared no better than its predecessor, and the scheme was quietly dropped. Meanwhile, other interests were still toying with the idea of a connecting link running south-eastwards from Alston to Frosterley, and a possible route was surveyed in the early 1870s. The suggested line would have involved substantial earthworks and fearsome gradients, and although a line was finally opened between Frosterley and Wearhead in 1895, the intervening section from Wearhead to Alston remained no more than a fascinating 'might have been'.

Alston Branch Bridges

The South Tyne valley had provided a viable route for the mid-19th century railway builders, but the need to cross subsidiary streams such as the Knar Burn ensured that the Alston branch was characterised by large numbers of bridges. Many of these structures have been referred to in Chapter Three, but readers may nevertheless be interested in some further details, and the following table therefore gives details relating to every bridge between Haltwhistle and Alston. The numbers given represent the official NER bridge numbering system, which remained in force until closure of the line in 1976.

Table 5

BRIDGES AND VIADUCTS ON THE ALSTON BRANCH

No.	Type	Arches	Widest span ft	m.	ch.	Notes
1	Public road bridge	1				Underbridge
2	Occupation bridge	1	6.5	00	24	Underbridge
3	River and occupation	6	53	00	40	South Tyne viaduct
4	Public road bridge	1	22	00	58	Underbridge
5	Occupation bridge	1	29	00	73	
6	Occupation bridge	1	29.5	01	43	
7	Timber footbridge	1	25	01	51	
8	Occupation bridge	1	25.25	01	58	
9	Public road bridge	1	29.25	02	43	Park bridge
10	Underline culvert	1	24	02	62	Park Burn bridge
11	Occupation bridge	3	26	02	72	Built of timber
12	Underline culvert	1	n/a	03	34	
13	Occupation bridge	1	25.33	03	49	
14	Underline culvert	1	4	04	27	
15	Occupation bridge	1	10	04	33	Underbridge
16	River bridge	18	58	04	55	Lambley viaduct
17	Occupation bridge	3	25	05	03	Built of timber
18	Occupation bridge	1	9	05	27	Underbridge
19	Underline culvert	1	4	05	35	
20	Occupation bridge	1	9.5	05	54	Underbridge
21	River bridge	5	20	05	67	Glendue Burn viaduct
22	Occupation bridge	1	8	06	05	Underbridge
23	Underline culvert	1	3	06	45	
24	Occupation bridge	1	24	06	54	Softley bridge
25	Occupation bridge	1	10	07	08	Underbridge
26	River bridge	6*	39	07	25	Thinhope Burn viaduct
27	Occupation bridge	1	4	07	42	Underbridge
28	Public road bridge	1	25	07	48	
29	Timber footbridge	3	24.33	07	67	
30	Occupation bridge	1	10	08	16	Underbridge
31	River and occupation	4	30	08	21	Knar Burn viaduct
32	Occupation bridge	1	25	08	33	
33	Occupation bridge	2	25	08	33	Slaggyford viaduct
34	Occupation bridge	1	25	08	69	
35	Occupation bridge	1	8	09	04	Underbridge
36	Underline culvert	1	3	09	14	
37	Occupation bridge	1	8	09	19	Underbridge
38	Underline culvert	1	3	09	29	
39	Public road bridge	1	25	09	42	Thornhope bridge
40	River bridge	4	30	09	56	Thornhope Burn viaduct
41	Occupation bridge	1	12	09	59	Underbridge
42	Occupation bridge	1	25	10	26	
43	Occupation bridge	1	15	10	48	Underbridge

* 5 open, one blank arch.

44	Underline culvert	1	2.5	10	50	
45	Underline culvert	1	2	10	51	
46	Occupation bridge	1	25	10	63	
47	Underline culvert	1	2.75	11	02	
48	River bridge	3	20	11	20	Lort Burn viaduct
49	Underline culvert	1	2	11	33	
50	Occupation bridge	1	8	11	35	Underbridge
51	River bridge	3	49	11	48	Gilderdale Burn viaduct
52	Occupation bridge	1	25	11	57	
53	Occupation bridge	1	6	11	79	Underbridge
54	Occupation bridge	1	8	12	12	Underbridge
55	Underline culvert	1	n/a			
56	Occupation bridge	1	n/a			
57	River bridge	3	39	12	50	Alston viaduct
58	Occupation bridge	1	8	12	56	Underbridge
59	Occupation bridge	1	4	12	61	Underbridge
60	Occupation bridge	1	7	12	75	Underbridge
61	Public road bridge	1	24 (?)	13	14	

NOTES

Unless otherwise stated, all bridges were built of stone. The names given in the 'notes' column are, in most cases, the official appellations used by BR. Local nomenclature may have been at variance in some instances — bridge 31, for instance, was sometimes called Barnesford bridge, while bridge 48 was also called Whitley Burn viaduct. Further confusion may result from the fact that the dimensions quoted were nominal, and minor distortions meant that the width of a given arch may be slightly different to the quoted figures.

The South Tyne viaduct at Haltwhistle had 6 spans, five of which had shew arches.
N.E. Stead Collection

Chapter Five

The British Railways Era (1948–1976)

The nationalisation of railways on 1st January, 1948 made little appreciable difference to rural branch lines such as the Haltwhistle to Alston route, and the late 1940s and early 1950s were, in most respects, merely a continuation of the LNER era. As on so many other lines, the only obvious change concerned the liveries of locomotives and rolling stock. The teak brown coach livery of the LNER was replaced by an overall maroon colour scheme, while 'mixed traffic' locomotives such as the 'G5' 0–4–4Ts were repainted in LNWR-style lined black livery.

Motive Power 1947–1959

The new liveries were, however, merely cosmetic, and in terms of motive power the Alston branch was still an 'NER' route — the ex-NER 'G5' 0–4–4 tanks being much in evidence around 1950. The regular engine at this time was 'G5' 0–4–4T No. 67315, though other 'G5' locomotives appeared sporadically, and these occasional performers included Nos. 62741 and 67277.

There were, after 1948, still two engines based at Alston, and in addition to the 'G5' there was also an 0–6–0 for goods work. The last 'J21' — No. 5100 — was transferred to Northallerton in 1948, and in its place Alston received Gresley 'J39' 0–6–0 No. 64851. The 'J39' 0–6–0s became familiar sights in the South Tyne Valley during the next few years, and in time they appeared on both passenger and freight workings. Several different 'J39s' ran on the branch during the 1950s, one of the most regular performers being No. 64814 which was noted on the branch on numerous occasions between 1953 and 1957. Other members of the class used on the line included Nos. 64705, 64842, 64849, 64812, 64816, 64858 and 64870.

In June 1953 Alston received an entirely new allocation in the form of Ivatt class '4MT' 2–6–0s Nos. 43126 and 43128; sister engine No. 43121 sometimes appeared when one or other of the regular engines was under repair. The use of these ex-LMS locomotives may have been something of an experiment, and in the event the Ivatt engines did not enjoy a monopoly of the Alston route. They were replaced by similar (but better-looking) British Railways standard class '3MTs' Nos. 77011 and 77014, while class '4MTs' Nos. 76049 and 76024 also appeared towards the end of steam operation. These modern engines did not, however, entirely supercede the massive-looking 'J39s', and in a sample week's running in the summer of 1957 the branch train was hauled by No. 64814 in place of the standard BR-built moguls on at least two occasions.

The sturdy 'J39s' were liked by train crews who appreciated their hauling power on the hilly Alston line, and perhaps for this reason the class tended to be used on freight workings while the mixed traffic 2–6–0s were typically employed on branch passenger trains. Paul Lefevre, who knew the area well during the 1950s, has recorded several visits to the branch during the period under review, and on these occasions the line seemed to be worked by a satisfying variety of motive power:

> 'G5' 0–4–4Ts and 'J21' 0–6–0s . . . were the types in use when I first visited the branch, the former on passenger work only, the latter being used for both passenger and goods . . . On my next visit to Haltwhistle, a 'J39' was waiting with the Alston train, although I was not able to journey along the branch to find out what other engine was in residence. From then on, visits became more commonplace and my very first journey over the line was behind an LMS class '4MT' 2–6–0, with a 'J39' (attached to an NER tender) performing the goods tasks. A few months later I travelled the branch twice in one week; the first behind the '4MT', with no sign of the second engine, the second behind a Standard class '3MT' 2–6–0, with the class '4MT' taking care of the goods. A visit by road to Alston came next, one Sunday, when in the shed was a 'J39' 0–6–0 and the class '3MT' 2–6–0 outside.
>
> A subsequent holiday in the area offered the chance to further my knowledge of the line, which was to me the most interesting in Britain. I was pulled from Haltwhistle to Alston behind a class '4MT' 2–6–0; at the terminus was the class '3MT' with the goods, and it was the '3MT' that took me back to the junction — the only function of the engine on the downhill run was to provide braking! Next day I again headed up the branch behind the '4MT', and the '3MT' was again shunting at Alston (and took the next passenger train) . . . I travelled up and down the branch many times that week behind the '3MT' and '4MT' moguls.

Mr Lefevre also mentioned that a fireman had talked of a 'large tanky' on the line; this may have been either a 'V1' 2–6–2T or an 'L1' 2–6–4T — though the unidentified engine could equally have been a Carlisle-based London Midland Region 2–6–4T. Other engines said to have been used on the Alston line during the BR era included a 'D20' 4–4–0 and an ex-LMS class '4F' 0–6–0 from Carlisle.

In general, tender engines reigned supreme on the branch after World War II, the usual types being the 'J39' 0–6–0s, and ex-LMS or BR moguls recalled by Mr Lefevre (see *Table 6*).

Table 6

TYPICAL MOTIVE POWER ON THE ALSTON BRANCH c.1900–1959

Class	*Wheel Arrangement*	*Sample Numbers*
G6	0–4–4T	69/319
G5	0–4–4T	405/1755/1795/1838 and 62741/67277/67315
F8	2–4–2T	172/1599
N8	0–6–2T	863
J21	0–6–0	51/5100/5101
J25	0–6–0	2101
J39	0–6–0	64705/64812/64814/64816/64849/64851/64858/64870
Ivatt 4MT	2–6–0	43121/43126/43128
BR 3MT	2–6–0	77011/77014
BR 4MT	2–6–0	76024/76049

Ironically, the use of tender engines for both passenger and goods workings coincided with the abandonment and subsequent removal of Alston's turntable. The table was out of use (but still *in situ*) in 1951, but it was later removed, and the platform line was then extended across the former turntable pit. These new arrangements did not provide any connection between the running line and the engine release road, and for this reason it was necessary for incoming trains to reverse out of the station in order to run-round. Neither did BR erect any buffer stops at the end of the lines that had hitherto connected with the turntable, and old sleepers were therefore laid across the rails to impede breakaways. It was usual, after the turntable had been taken out of use, for engines to run with their chimneys facing Alston so that all tender-first running would take place in the up direction (i.e. downhill towards Haltwhistle).

Post-War Train Services

The post-war train service was similar to that in operation prior to 1939, and there were, by the early 1950s, seven or eight trains in each direction. The September 1951 working timetable shows that the first up service left Alston at 5.25 am and reached Haltwhistle at 5.58; this was primarily a workmen's service and it did not call at any of the intermediate stations. The return working left Haltwhistle at 6.14 am and reached Alston by 6.53 am, calling *en route* at all of the branch stations to pick up workmen.

At 7.10 am the next up working departed from Alston, and it was common practice for this train to be double-headed so that the Alston goods engine could reach Haltwhistle without recourse to light engine movements. The returning 8 am service arrived back in Alston at 8.39 am, and there were further return trips from Alston to the junction at 8.55, 10.42 am and 2.00 pm. Meanwhile, a goods train had left Alston at 2.40 pm, and this freight working called at all of the intermediate stations in the course of a leisurely trip down the valley to Haltwhistle. The goods reached Lambley at 3.07 pm and remained on the Lambley Fell line until 3.50 pm — allowing the 3.25 pm down passenger service to clear the single line section. The 2.40 pm goods was worked by the Alston goods engine that had earlier worked through to Haltwhistle in conjunction with the 7.10 am passenger train, and in order for this locomotive to arrive back in Alston prior to working the 2.40 pm it was customary for one of the down passenger services — usually the 11.45 am ex-Haltwhistle — to be piloted by the goods locomotive.

The pick-up goods finally reached Haltwhistle at 4.22 pm, and at 4.25 pm a further passenger train departed from Alston. This train, which carried school children to their homes in the South Tyne Valley, reached Haltwhistle at 5.04 pm and returned to Alston at 5.40, reaching the terminus by 6.19 pm. In the interim, the goods engine had itself set off back to Alston at 5.05 pm, and after calling intermediately at Featherstone Park and Coanwood the returning freight train reached Lambley at 5.39 pm. After shunting on the Lambley Fell branch for 40 minutes, the journey to Alston resumed at 6.20 pm, and the pick-up freight arrived back in Alston by 6.38 pm (having been overtaken by the 5.40 pm passenger service which left Lambley at 5.56 pm while the goods engine was busily shunting the colliery line).

The final weekday up service left Alston at 6.50 pm and arrived back at the terminus by 8.49 pm. On Saturdays, an additional evening working ran from Alston to Haltwhistle at 9.05 pm and returned from the junction at

10.10 pm — this last down service being heavily used by Saturday night revellers returning from drinking sessions in Haltwhistle.

The branch was worked in two shifts, and in the mid-1950s the guards' shifts ran from 5.15 am to 1.15 pm, and from 1.15 pm until 9.15 pm. On Saturdays the day shift guard commenced work at the slightly later time of 6.15 am, while the late shift guard started work at 8.35 am. These altered times allowed the heavily-loaded Saturday trains to be run with two guards — one man manning the brake compartment while his colleague collected the fares aboard the train.

The passenger vehicles employed at this time were of various kinds, and although venerable ex-NER stock still appeared, some trains were formed of vestibuled ex-LNER coaches in British Railways red and cream livery. At other times, vehicles from more distant parts of the former London & North Eastern system unexpectedly appeared, and in this context it is interesting to note that ex-Great Eastern coaches were not unknown on the Alston branch after World War II. The coaches involved were corridor vehicles which enabled guards to walk through the train collecting fares; they were not, however, permanent allocations, and these GER veterans were replaced by LNER corridor stock.

The Slow Decline

The Alston branch ran through an area of scattered rural communities that had never produced much passenger traffic, and although coal and minerals provided at least some bulk freight traffic, it is likely that the branch was never more than marginally profitable. In the days when railway companies such as the North Eastern Railway had enjoyed a monopoly of land transport, branch lines like the Alston route were tolerated because they acted as useful 'feeders' for the main line network — it was, moreover, possible for profits from more important parts of the system to be used to subsidise less-profitable routes; as we have seen, the Alston line was rationalised during the LNER era when its intermediate stations were down-graded in various ways — and this process continued unabated after World War II. Featherstone Park and Coanwood, for example, lost their goods facilities in August 1954 and September 1955 respectively, while at the same time the private sidings that had formerly served local mines and quarries were progressively removed as mineral deposits became exhausted and economic changes took their toll.

Lambley and Slaggyford retained their goods yards throughout the 1950s, but the reprieve was only temporary, and both stations lost their freight handling facilities in September 1960. The Lambley Fell line had succumbed only a few weeks earlier, and with its demise Alston remained the only station capable of handling coal and mineral traffic.

Meanwhile, the railway continued to serve the people of South Tynedale, and although, in 1959, there were suggestions that the line might become a candidate for closure, local travellers were confident that their line would be retained as a vital lifeline during the winter months. On 9th December, 1959 the North Eastern Transport Users' Consultative Committee reported that BR had agreed to keep the branch in operation because there was no suitable road link along the South Tyne Valley.

Dieselisation

In November 1959 BR introduced a diesel-worked passenger timetable, and this led, in turn, to the closure of Alston engine shed. At the same time, the snow plough that had hitherto been stationed at Alston for winter use was moved to Newcastle. The last scheduled steam-hauled passenger train pulled into Alston station (carrying 'Royal Train' headlights) on the evening of Saturday 27th September, 1959. This was not quite the end of steam operation because remaining freight services were still steam-hauled, and steam engines were still available for use in the event of a diesel failure. In the summer of 1960, for example, Paul Lefevre again visited the Alston line, and was delighted to find that the branch train consisted of two Gresley corridor coaches and one ex-LMS non-corridor vehicle, hauled by 'an exceptionally clean '4MT' 2–6–0'; the failed diesel multiple unit could be seen lurking in a siding at Haltwhistle 'in total disgrace'! (It appeared that the class '4MT' had been rostered to work the branch goods service, but it had evidently been pressed into emergency passenger service when the dmu failed at Haltwhistle.)

Local freight services to and from Alston were worked by Carlisle-based locomotives, and Carlisle shed was also responsible for the provision of a light engine which ran over the branch at night during periods of snow, in order that the line could be kept free from snow drifts. Such precautions were certainly needed during the severe winter of 1963 when — as in 1947 — the Alston branch again became a vital lifeline in appalling weather conditions. On one occasion, the railway was instrumental in saving the life of a seriously ill man who could not be evacuated from Lambley by ambulance; a doctor was able to reach the casualty by rail, and the sick man was later taken to Haltwhistle on the evening train. He was then transferred into a waiting ambulance and taken to hospital in Carlisle, where he received emergency treatment.

The railway was kept running throughout the 1963 emergency because dedicated employees such as Mrs Middleton braved the atrocious conditions in order to reach their posts, and it is pleasing to record that Mary Middleton was one of a number of people chosen by a national newspaper to spend a holiday weekend in London as a way of thanking them for their dedicated service during the early weeks of 1963.

Towards Closure

Steam was replaced, at Alston, by Metro Cammell two car sets (later class '101s') and in the next few years these good looking and relatively comfortable diesel multiple units became familiar sights in the scenic South Tyne Valley. In theory, the flexibility of multiple unit operation should have allowed BR to introduce a much-improved timetable, but this did not happen on the Alston line, and there were, in the diesel era, no more than six or seven workings each way between Haltwhistle and Alston. In May

1971, for instance, there were departures from Haltwhistle to Alston at 6.19, 8.19 am, 12 noon, 3.34, 5.42 and 8.30 pm. In the reverse direction, balancing up services left Alston at 6.58, 8.58 am, 12.55, 4.13, 6.50 and 9.09 pm respectively. An additional train ran on Saturdays, and this provided an extra round trip from Haltwhistle at 10.15 pm, with a corresponding return journey from Alston at 10.53 pm.

Unfortunately, the positive aspects of dieselisation were not exploited to their fullest potential, and whereas in Germany (or other advanced nations) modernisation was seen as a means of getting more people on to the railways, BR succeeded only in driving customers onto the roads in ever-increasing numbers. It is staggering, for example, to find that most forms of cheap day return tickets were abolished coincidently with dieselisation, and for this reason fares doubled on the day that the new multiple units entered regular service. Local travellers became convinced that their line was being run down prior to closure — and this belief was reinforced by the sight of boarded stations and acres of derelict sidings; by 1962 the line was said to be 'losing' £6,000 a year. Neither did the form taken by modernisation on the Alston branch lead to appreciable savings, and there was considerable wastage involved in regular empty stock workings to and from South Gosforth or Hexham at the start and end of each day's service (one wonders, for example, why the branch set could not have been stationed at Haltwhistle, with consequent savings in terms of fuel consumption)?

Perhaps the worst blow, in the run-up to closure, came in 1960 when the Anglo-Austral Mines of Nenthead decided to send their mineral products out of the area by road. What little goods traffic then remained was handled at Alston until September 1965, but thereafter the line became a passenger-only route, with a simple shuttle service worked entirely by diesel units.

The withdrawal of goods services enabled BR to introduce further cost-cutting measures, and the line was reduced to one-engine-in-steam working in 1966. The signal boxes at Coanwood, Lambley and Alston were taken out of use, and the level crossings at Featherstone Park and Slaggyford were reduced to the status of 'open' crossings without gates or barriers; at Coanwood, the gates remained in place, but as no signalman was in attendance the crossing was operated by train crews. Most of the line's signals were removed, although fixed distants were retained in certain places; at Featherstone Park, for example, an old NER slotted post distant remained *in situ* — its yellow arm permanently fixed in the 'caution' position.

Further rationalisation resulted in the lifting of most pointwork and connections between Haltwhistle and Alston, leaving a loop siding in place on the down side at Alston. This siding was intended for emergency use (perhaps during inclement weather), but its retention ensured that the terminus still had a run-round facility, and the branch did not become a complete 'basic railway'. The tablet pouch was still carried by train crews, and an attached key enabled them to unlock the residual pointwork at the Alston end of the line.

Alston station had lost its overall roof by the early 1970s, and with the engine shed and associated trackwork all removed, travellers arrived and departed from a somewhat bleak open platform. On the other hand, the substantial Jacobean style station buildings remained intact, and with station buildings still extant at Slaggyford and Lambley, the branch retained much of its Victorian atmosphere. Some of the intermediate stopping places were still equipped with ornate glass platform lamps — although Featherstone Park and Coanwood lost their wooden booking offices and waiting rooms.

The withdrawal of goods services and de-signalling of the branch resulted in a significant reduction in the number of people needed to operate the line, and in its last years the route was worked by guards based at Hexham and footplate staff from South Gosforth, together with a handful of permanent way men — among them Mr George Watson (who retired a few weeks prior to closure). George Kipling and Peter Huntsman were among the last guards employed on the line, and both have recorded their impressions of the railway at the end of its working life. George Kipling recalled that:

> We had dmu trains on the branch all the time, after steam finished, and until the line was finally closed. We collected fares from the time the diesels started — that was an extra job, and the rest of the work was general guard's duty. All rules were carried out as on a main line; mail, parcels, and letters were carried to each station, but after the stations became halts there was nothing at all, and the guards did everything, collecting fares as conductors, looking after passengers, etc. If there were any sheep or cattle straying on the line the guard got them off into the fields again. I worked on the branch, operating from Hexham for about 22 years — that was 2 weeks on the branch and 2 weeks together on the Carlisle–Newcastle line (per month).

In similar vein, Peter Huntsman's recollections provide an interesting insight into the final years of operation between 1956 and 1976:

> I started work on the line when the steam trains were withdrawn and for several years trains were worked by Hexham drivers. This appeared to be fairly economical, but it did not last, and the work was later taken over by Gosforth drivers. This resulted in a lot of men travelling 'passenger', and added to the running costs of the line.
>
> As often happens on branch lines, many people only used the trains when the weather was bad and they were unable to use their cars. Many of the trains were almost empty, especially in winter. The passengers who used the line on a regular basis were very friendly, and of course everyone was known by their first names. They were, as you often find in the country districts, very honest. I once paid a passenger's fare as she only had a £5 note, and it was two weeks later when she paid me the fare — I had forgotten all about it!
>
> After some years BR decided to effect some economies, and the level crossings became unmanned. When this took place road traffic had the right of way. The train driver had to stop and make sure no road traffic was close before we crossed the road. We had one or two near misses but I don't think any accident actually happened.
>
> When the pick-up goods train from Carlisle stopped running the diesel multiple units hauled 'vanfits' all the way to Alston, where they were loaded up with golf club heads manufactured by a firm in the town (Precision Products). They were transferred to a parcel train at Haltwhistle.

Thinking of the severe weather encountered in the early months of 1963, Mr Huntsman referred to the railway's fine record of uninterrupted service to the community:

In spite of all the winter weather, I don't think the line was ever closed by snow in the time I worked on it, and in severe conditions the railway was the *only* way into Alston. I made many good friends on the line, and it was a very sad day when I stepped off at Haltwhistle for the last time.

These sentiments were echoed by former driver Alan Robinson, who worked on the branch throughout the British Railways period, and was able to give a very full picture of the line during its final years of operation:

The Alston branch was a very busy line when I was promoted to driver, having two engines — a 'J21' and a 'G5', which were changed every week to ten days (for boiler wash outs and repairs) by engines from Blaydon shed, the changeover taking place at Haltwhistle.

I came from a railway family, my father was a driver at Hexham, the family having over 200 years railway service. I was in 'digs' at Alston for two years before I was able to get a house and move my family from Hexham to Alston. When I arrived at Alston I was made welcome and became part of the life on the branch. I spent twelve happy years until diesel replaced steam in November 1959, when once again I returned to Hexham — but was still in touch with the branch as Hexham men worked most of the units until it was itself closed. I was then moved to Gosforth, but once again found myself working the Alston branch and continued to do so until the final closure in 1976.

I soon found out that the passengers on the branch were friends. There were many different 'stops' at wayside cottages and farms to allow them to alight and save a long walk from a station to their homes. My fireman was Maurice Peart, and we were together for eight years until he moved to Hartlepool to become a driver.

Severe winters often meant that the only way into Alston was by rail, and the farmers would then bring their milk to the stations to be moved to the dairy at Carlisle (or elsewhere); bread and groceries were brought to the stations from Haltwhistle, and everyone joined in to load and unload the vans.

As the years went by the changes began, and these were the forerunners of the decline of the railway; first from four sets of men to three, then from two engines to one until in November 1959 the final blow came when the steam engine was replaced by diesel. Though I considered myself lucky to stay with the branch until its closure, the passenger traffic was declining, but we were still able to help travellers as we had done in steam days.

Mr Robinson recounted two incidents that had taken place during his years of service on the branch — one of which involved his friend and colleague Frank Birkett, who had the misfortune to fall out of a train at Coanwood:

One very sad event marred my time at Alston. When working the 6.50 pm evening train from Alston to Haltwhistle, the guard, Frank Birkett had an accident. We were approaching Coanwood station when my fireman . . . shouted that Frankie had fallen out of the guard's van. I ran along the platform and found him partly under the last coach. I thought that he had lost a leg, but on pulling him out I found that this was not so. I got him into the train and 'phoned Haltwhistle to have an ambulance waiting. He was taken to hospital, and after a few months he was able to return to work, but was never the same man and he died the following year.

The other incident recalled by Mr Robinson occurred during the winter of 1963:

I was conducting a light diesel engine with a snow plough, and running in front of the diesel unit. On arrival at Alston the driver and second man went for a cup of tea. I was standing on the platform when a coffin was carried through the barrier ready to be taken to Newcastle Crematorium. Thinking it would save time I told them to load the coffin into the diesel cab, but when the crew returned and found a corpse in their cab they refused to get on the engine, so I had to get help to get the coffin back onto the platform.

Railbuses and Special Trains

Although class '101' multiple units were the mainstay of Alston branch operation between 1959 and 1976, it would be fitting to mention that, in May 1965, German-built 4-wheeled railbus No. E79964 was sent north for trials on the Alston branch. Sister vehicle No. E79963 arrived in August, but it did not remain for long, and No. E79964 was left to carry on alone until the following winter. Built by Waggon und Maschinenbau in 1958, these German railbuses were part of a batch of five ordered under the BR modernisation plan; they were 41ft 10in. long and could accommodate 56 passengers. They had a small driver's compartment at each end, and passengers entered the vehicles through centrally-placed sliding doors on either side.

In theory, the railbus idea should have solved many of the problems associated with the operation of lightly-used rural lines such as the Alston route, but sadly, the experiment was a fiasco. Like other 4-wheeled passenger vehicles, the railbuses were susceptible to vibration as they lurched and yawed their way along jointed track, and some travellers complained about rough riding. Moreover, the units were plagued by mechanical problems, and their heaters were unreliable during the depths of winter. Further problems stemmed from their inability to haul other vehicles, while there were also difficulties with refuelling, which could only be carried out in South Gosforth.

In retrospect, the railbus experiment failed for a number of reasons — the most obvious being that the 4-wheeled vehicles ordered from Waggon und Maschinenbau (and several British manufacturers) were too light and underpowered to give satisfactory service in British conditions; larger, bogie vehicles such as the Metro-Cammell class '101s' were, on the other hand, ideal for use on lines such as the Alston route, and these units soon returned to the branch.

The use of railbuses on the Alston branch introduced an element of variety into daily operations that would otherwise have been lacking, but of even greater interest to enthusiasts was the occasional appearance of steam-hauled specials during these last years of operation. On Monday 27th March, 1967, for instance, the Branch Line Society joined forces with the Stephenson Locomotive Society and the Scottish Locomotive Preservation Society to run the 'Scottish Rambler No. 6' railtour over lines in Scotland and the north of England. The tour — which lasted over an entire Easter holiday weekend — ended with an afternoon trip from Carlisle to Alston, the motive power, on this occasion, being Ivatt class '4MT' 2–6–0 No. 43121.

Closure of the Line

The harsh winters of 1947 and 1963 had demonstrated that the Alston branch fulfilled a vital role in times of heavy snowfalls and sustained low temperatures, but the 1960s were nevertheless the 'Beeching era', and at a time when the government was making no secret of its hostility towards the nationalised railways, the future for loss-making branch lines such as the Alston route was bleak. In 1962, however, the North Eastern area Transport Users' Consultative Committee again reported that severe hardship would result from any closure of the railway, and in 1964 a change of government brought an end to the era of mass railway closures.

The railway trade unions predicted that the incoming Labour government would herald a period of stability for the state-owned railways, and in 1967 Mrs Barbara Castle presented a blueprint for future development, which envisaged a 'basic railway network' of some 11,000 route miles. Although some closures were still contemplated, the so-called Castle Plan was much better than the final Beeching proposals which (if fully implemented) would have reduced the BR system to no more than 3,000 route miles. Unfortunately, the new Labour scheme placed many lines serving rural (and predominantly Tory) areas outside of the basic network, and although the Transport Act of 1968 paved the way for government support for socially-necessary services, the Castle Plan did little to help the Alston branch — which was *not* considered to be part of the basic network.

In December 1969 Mr Fred Mulley, the then Minister of Transport, announced that the Alston branch would receive grant aid of £43,000 under Section 39 of the 1968 Transport Act, but this aid was provisional, and could not be justified 'for a period longer than two years'. In the event, the branch was the recipient of further grants which, by 1973, had reached £72,000 per annum. Meanwhile, British Railways had made a further closure proposal, and this new proposal was considered by the Transport Users' Consultative Committee at a public meeting held at Alston in March 1971. It was revealed that Alston was used by just 20–30 travellers a day, while some of the smaller stations were hardly used at all. Surveys carried out at Coanwood, for instance, showed that about 14 people travelled regularly to and from Haltwhistle, but there were very few travellers in the opposite direction between Coanwood and Alston. In general, there appeared to be around 60 regular users who relied on the railway to get to work or to go shopping, while there were another 152 casual users, including about 50 old age pensioners.

The surveys were undertaken in representative weeks in August and October, but the census figures gave no indication of the extent to which people flocked to the railway during adverse weather conditions, and in opposing the proposed closure, Northumberland County Council pointed out that about 360 people travelled by road from Alston to Haltwhistle each weekday. Although it did not necessarily follow that all of these people would travel by train if the weather was bad, it was clear that — in the event of a total blockage — the railway would provide a useful alternative means of getting to work. The Council also pointed out that many road users preferred to travel by train when the roads were made hazardous by black ice — and such conditions occurred frequently throughout the course of a normal winter.

The arguments against closure were concerned primarily with the problems experienced during adverse weather conditions — although some objectors suggested that the Alston area was growing in importance as a tourist destination, and in this context Mr M.A. Seymour of the English Lakes Counties Travel Association presented some apposite facts and figures; he pointed out that Alston had a population of about 2,200, but this figure frequently doubled between May and September when hikers, ramblers and other holidaymakers visited the town. While admitting that it would be difficult to estimate how many of Alston's summer visitors arrived by rail, Mr Seymour suggested that holidaymakers travelling by train would, in the main, have travelled a greater distance — thereby paying BR a 'good deal more than just the fare for the Haltwhistle–Alston section'. He added that many of Alston's summer visitors were in the 15–19 age group, and these younger people would not be car owners.

Other objectors included Cumberland County Council, Haltwhistle Rural District Council, Alston Rural District Council and the Northern Rural Development Board, while several local residents submitted individual objections to the proposed closure.

Having considered the evidence for and against closure, the Transport Users' Consultative Committee (TUCC) eventually decided that severe hardship would be caused if the railway was closed, and it was recommended that the closure should be deferred until the problem of new roads had been resolved. In reaching this conclusion, the Committee admitted that the number of people who would suffer as a result of closure would not be great, but at the same time they considered the geographical problems such as steep hills and narrow roads made the Alston branch a special case to which normal financial considerations could not be applied.

The outcome of the 1971 TUCC hearing seemed to guarantee the railway's survival — at least for the foreseeable future — but in January 1973 the government announced that the closure would be implemented, subject to the provision of an improved road link between Alston and Haltwhistle. Explaining this decision, the Department of the Environment claimed that earnings from fares totalled just £4,000, whereas the cost of the service 'as estimated for the purpose of grant' was £77,000; this meant (claimed the DoE) that the branch was 'losing' £73,000 a year. The one crumb of comfort for local travellers was the fact that closure would be delayed until May 1975, allowing time for the necessary road link to be built.

Although the government was unwilling to spend £73,000 a year to keep the railway in operation, the Treasury was keen to spend the much greater sum of £300,000 on an 'all weather' road link to Haltwhistle. This led to suggestions that the money that was on offer from central government might be spent on buying the branch in its entirety, and with these thoughts in mind Lord Ridley, the Chairman of Northumberland County Council, urged that the branch should be bought from BR and then leased to the newly-formed South Tynedale Railway Preservation Society. This novel idea seemed, at the time, to offer a way forward for the Alston branch (and also for other threatened rural services), but regrettably, the government refused to transfer money from road works to railway preservation, and the expensive 'all weather' road plan was put into effect.

Work on the new road proceeded apace, and with completion scheduled for May 1976, BR decided that the Alston branch would be closed on 3rd May, 1976. As this was a Monday, the last trains would run on Saturday 1st May, and the operating authorities prepared themselves for a vast influx of last day travellers as the fateful day approached.

The Last Train

Saturday 1st May, 1976 was a sombre, wet day, but the depressing weather did not deter an estimated 5,000 people from travelling north to ride on the last scheduled passenger services. Alston station was decorated with flags and bunting, and members of the South Tynedale Railway Preservation Society (who were still hoping to revive the branch as a private venture) turned out in force to distribute publicity material and man a shop that had been opened in the station buildings. Teas and light refreshments were available at the station, while in Alston itself, the 'Friends of Alston Town Hall' served tea and coffee to raise funds in aid of the Town Hall restoration fund.

The doomed line was exceptionally busy throughout the day, prompting a BR official to remark that 'normal passenger levels were much, much lower — only at the end had people realised just how nice the line was'. The normal trains were filled to capacity, while hundreds of others travelled over the branch in special trains, one of which — 'The Alston Farewell' — had run through from Newcastle; organised by the Stephenson Locomotive Society, this train had left Newcastle at 11 am, the fare from Tyneside to Alston (and return via other local lines) being just £3.25.

The guard, on this final morning, was George Kipling, and he was surprised to find that people had travelled from all over the country to say farewell to the Alston line; some had journeyed from as far as the South Coast to participate in the sad, but historic occasion (an indication that the fight to retain the South Tynedale branch had reached national proportions). Mr Kipling went back to Hexham when his shift was over, but after tea he returned to Haltwhistle to ride on the line for the last time. His colleague Peter Huntsman was working the afternoon shift, and Mr Kipling and Mr Huntsman were both welcomed by loud cheers as they joined the train.

Some people rode up and down the line for two or more trips, but finally, at 9.09 pm, the time came for the last train to commence its melancholy journey from Alston to Haltwhistle. This was indeed the end, and as the brightly-lit multiple unit formation pulled out of the packed terminus, two pipers played a lament; one of them was Mr Arthur Middleton, the son of former signalwoman Mary Middleton and a member of the Newton Aycliffe Pipe Band. A barrage of detonators echoed round the town as the last train accelerated into the night, while those aboard the train peered into the darkness as the familiar landmarks glided dimly by for the last time.

The train was greeted by little groups of people as it paused at the intermediate stations at Slaggyford, Lambley, Coanwood and Featherstone, and guard Peter Huntsman noted that 'many of the old folks who had travelled on the line all their lives' were in tears when they stepped off the train at Haltwhistle. The final journey came to an end at about 9.45 pm, and as the last day travellers dispersed by car and train, everybody was conscious that 123 years of railway history had drawn to a close.

Class 'J39' 0–6–0 No. 64814 waits at Alston with the 6.50 pm evening train to Haltwhistle, on 24th August, 1954. Engines always ran tender-first towards Haltwhistle after the turntable at Alston was taken out of use. *R.F. Roberts*

L.N.E.R | L.N.E.R
015 | 015
COANWOOD to LAMBLEY | LAMBLEY to COANWOOD
Via | Via
Available within ... of date of issue | Available on day of issue only.
FIRST | R | FIRST
Fare s. d. For conditions see back. | Fare s. d. For conditions see back.

L. N. E. R. | L. N. E. R.
9376 | 9376
FURLOUGH | FURLOUGH
FEATHERSTONE TO HALTWHISTLE | HALTWHISTLE TO FEATHERSTONE PARK
Via | Via
Available for THREE months from date of issue | Available for THREE months from date of issue
THIRD For conditions see back | Fur. Rtn. 3211 | THIRD For conditions see back

Chapter Six

The South Tynedale Railway and Other Narrow Gauge Lines

The so-called 'all weather' road was opened by Lord Ridley on Monday 3rd May, its inauguration coinciding with the withdrawal of train services between Alston and Haltwhistle; the road link had cost much more than the £300,000 offered by the government in 1973, and the final bill was no less than £620,000. Those who had formerly travelled by train throughout the year were not convinced that the 'all weather' road would suffice during the depths of a Pennine winter, and sure enough, the first snows of winter soon exposed the pitiful deficiencies of road transport. The new link itself was kept clear (at some cost), but the real problems appeared on connecting roads — especially at Lintley bank, near the 10 mile post on the abandoned railway. Snow fell heavily during the week of 10th–15th January, and the road was blocked by 8 ft drifts by Thursday 13th January. The route was partially cleared by Saturday 15th, but a snowblower did not appear until the 18th, and in the meantime many local commuters were forced to stay at home.

This first railwayless winter brought home to Alston people what it meant to be cut off, and one embittered ex-railway traveller pointed out that incompetent bureaucrats and mediocre politicians had put the clock back a thousand years as far as the South Tyne Valley was concerned (traffic had been halted by a thin covering of snow in December, yet in pre-railway days horses had, he claimed, been able to pick their way through drifts of 2–3 ft).

Demolition of the Branch

There were still, at this time, hopes that the South Tynedale Railway Preservation Society would be able to revive the line as a viable transport link between Alston and Haltwhistle, and indeed a concerted campaign had been launched to prevent British Rail from lifting the track. A group of Labour MPs lobbied the Department of the Environment in an eleventh hour attempt to save the line, while Lord Ridley campaigned tirelessly on behalf of Northumberland County Council.

Many people hoped that BR would hand over the line to the local authorities, who would in turn lease it to the preservationists, but BR claimed that the abandoned route was worth £160,000 — and refused to let the South Tynedale Preservation Society operate the line until the track had been purchased. This unhelpful decision meant that the preservation group was unable to raise money by actually running the branch, and in the meantime scrap men started demolishing the line between Haltwhistle and Gilderdale Viaduct.

As the work of destruction continued, those who still wished to save the line could only watch helplessly as gradient posts, lineside huts, and Victorian station lanterns were ruthlessly swept away. The rails were removed between Haltwhistle and Gilderdale during the winter of 1976–77, much of the lifted material being sent to Inverkeithing for re-rolling. Many of the discarded chairs were despatched to a buyer in Holland, while the sleepers were initially left *in situ*. By March 1977, many of the latter had been cut into short sections for resale to the National Coal Board, though some individual sleepers were sold for about £3 each for use as gateposts or support beams. (The line had been partly relaid with concrete sleepers, but these sold for just £1 each, and one report suggested that many were simply discarded.)

The 1½ mile section of line between Alston and Gilderdale Burn was left in place until 14th March, 1977 in order to give the South Tynedale Railway Company time to raise the £40,800 purchase price demanded by BR for this residual part of the route. Sadly, the money could not be raised in time, and although the March deadline was subsequently extended, the lifting of this final section of track began in June.

Narrow Gauge Plans

The early months of 1977 were a black time for the South Tynedale Railway Society, and having failed in their attempt to rescue the line as a 13 mile working railway, the preservationists were obliged to wind up a company that had earlier been formed to work the line. The preservation group nevertheless remained in being, and with a strong body of support still in favour of some form of railway provision at Alston, the members eventually came to the conclusion that a narrow gauge line might be built from Alston to the county boundary at Gilderdale. It was pointed out that narrow gauge permanent way cost much less than standard gauge materials, while smaller, lighter equipment would obviously be much easier to lay and maintain. The proposed narrow gauge line would be no substitute for a full size railway between Alston and Haltwhistle, but in an area of growing tourist potential it was felt that a 2 ft gauge, steam-operated line would fulfil an entirely different need — and of course Alston's historic railway station would still be preserved as a tangible reminder of the branch line that had now gone.

Much remained to be done before the narrow gauge scheme could be implemented and in particular the society was still faced with a major problem in terms of land purchase. Fortunately, Cumbria County Council was amenable to the idea of buying the station site from BR, and purchase of the Cumbrian section of the trackbed was completed by 16th February, 1979. In an atmosphere of renewed enthusiasm, preservation society members adapted the former ladies' waiting room for use as a museum and visitor centre, and in August 1979 the first 2 ft gauge locomotive was delivered to Alston station; the new arrival was a 4-wheeled Hibberd diesel with a Ford 4-cylinder engine.

In the next few months, the preservation society transformed Alston station into an attractive tourist centre, and by 1982 the redeveloped site provided a variety of facilities for the public. The original 1852 station buildings stood at the centre of the new complex, and formed an appropriate headquarters for the South Tynedale Society; the ground floor was adapted for use as a shop and visitor centre, while staff rooms and toilets were available in a rebuilt extension at the north end of the building. Nearby, the stone goods shed survived intact as part of a building contractor's yard, and a corner of the former goods yard continued in use as a coal yard – a function it had fulfilled since the 1850s!

The area once occupied by Alston engine shed was transformed into a landscaped open space providing car parking and picnic areas beside the River Nent, and a small site at the southern extremity of the station was set aside for future museum use. The narrow gauge track layout consisted of a conventional run-round loop with a short spur at the southern end, and there were plans for an engine shed and repair shop to the north of the picnic area. The remaining part of the former station site was occupied by a factory unit, and the redeveloped station was thereby sub-divided into a variety of useful facilities, offering both industrial and leisure opportunities. Much valuable work on the South Tynedale part of the site had been carried out by a team funded by the Manpower Services Commission, though many hours of volunteer labour had also been expended on the South Tynedale project by ordinary STRPS members.

The first section of the STR was opened to public traffic on 30th July, 1983, and a weekend service was maintained throughout the summer. A second 4-wheeled diesel locomotive was ready in time for the 1984 season, and the first steam engine purchased by the Society arrived at Alston on 11th April, 1984.

Further progress was made in October 1987 when the South Tynedale Railway Preservation Society obtained a Light Railway Order for the 1½ miles of the line between Alston and Gilderdale; regular passenger services had already commenced over the new section, the first public service having been started in December 1986 (shortly after the section had been passed by the Department of Transport). The line ended beside a simple halt, but there were plans for an extension beyond the existing northern terminus at Gilderdale, and in 1986 the Society obtained planning permission for a further 3 mile section between Gilderdale and Slaggyford.

The South Tynedale Railway went from strength to strength throughout the 1980s, and with help from local authorities, the English Tourist Board and the Manpower Services Commission the project became an established part of the Alston scene. Ironically, the revived railway was soon carrying more passengers over its 1½ miles of line between Alston and Gilderdale than its standard gauge predecessor had carried in the Edwardian years, and whereas in the period 1900-1949 Alston station had booked around 13,350 passengers per annum, it was handling about 15,000 visitors a year during the 1980s. In 1987, for instance, the South Tynedale line carried 15,864 passengers.

The narrow gauge line was worked by a variety of locomotives, among them Henschel 0-4-0T No. 6 *Thomas Edmondson*, a former Imperial German Army standard locomotive dating from 1918. The locomotive stock in 1988 comprised no less than nine engines. The majority of these locomotives were industrial diesels, but it became the practice for visiting steam engines to be used on the line during the peak summer operating season.

The carriage stock available in the summer of 1988 included three covered vehicles, two of which had side doors while the third was entered via end vestibules. In common with other narrow gauge lines, the South Tynedale Railway also needed a small fleet of permanent way vehicles, and when, in the Autumn of 1987, British Gas installed a new gas main alongside the railway, it was possible for the South Tynedale Railway to provide a useful 'construction train' consisting of No. 8 *The Peril* and a rake of permanent way wagons.

The Railway Today

The South Tynedale Railway has continued to see considerable variety in terms of motive power, the permanent fleet being assisted and supplemented by visiting engines including Kerr Stuart 0-4-0T *Peter Pan*, Bagnall 0-4-0ST *Woto* and Hunslet 0-4-0ST *Jonathan*. In 1998, the line's annual September Gala gave visitors the opportunity to ride behind the Welsh Highland Railway's Bagnall 0-4-2T *Gelert*, as well as Henschel 0-4-0T *Helen Kathryn* and Hunslet 0-4-2T *Chaka's Kraal No. 6* - the latter engine being a long-term visitor to the line. Other visiting locomotives have included the West Lancashire Railway's Hunslet 0-4-0ST *Irish Mail*, and a steam tram engine from Telford.

Some of these 2 ft gauge engines were of comparatively small size, though others were of more substantial appearance. One of the most impressive locomotives seen on the South Tynedale route in recent years was a Polish 0-6-0WT, known as *Naklo*; this engine was built at Chrzanow in 1957, and has become No. 10 in the STR locomotive fleet.

Gilderdale remained the northern terminus of the line for many years, although it had been suggested that Slaggyford would have made an appropriate destination. In the meantime, work proceeded on a northwards extension from Gilderdale to Kirkhaugh, and it was hoped that this new section of narrow gauge line would be ready for opening in July 1998. The Kirkhaugh extension was finally opened on 4th September, 1999, the inaugural working being hauled by Hunslet 0-4-2T *Chaka's Kraal No. 6*. The extended line gave the railway an operating length of 2½ miles.

The September opening was followed by an 'official' opening on 29th June, 2000, motive power, on this occasion, being provided by Hudswell Clarke 0-6-0 diesel No. 4 *Naworth*. Future plans include an extension northwards to Slaggyford, some two miles further on. The South Tynedale railway already owns the trackbed between Kirkhaugh and the proposed terminus, and a Light Railway Order has been obtained. At the time of writing the railway terminates at Kirkhaugh, but it is hoped that the route will be extended to Slaggyford in due course.

It is perhaps, a happy coincidence, that the gauge chosen for the South Tynedale Railway was already well-established in the South Tyne valley - in fact, there is evidence to suggest that 2 ft gauge lines had been used in local lead mines during the industrial revolution. Iron rails had been introduced oil these lines by 1816, and it is recorded that, by 1817, some of the underground tramways had been extended beyond the mines to serve nearby washing floors and smelt mills.

The history of these lines is obscure, but it is known that some of the local mineral lines ran across country for considerable distances, and it would be worth saying a little more about those lines that have left visible remains - the most obvious candidate for further examination being the narrow gauge line which formerly ran eastwards from Coanwood station to reach collieries in the area to the east of the railway.

Tramways at Coanwood

Coanwood collieries have already been mentioned, but it is worth repeating that the Coanwood area was a very old coal mining area, and there are numerous references to coal mining in the immediate vicinity. The North of England Institute of Mining & Mechanical Engineers has a plan of

Coanwood Colliery dating from the late 18th century, together with several accounts of borings carried out at various times between 1762 and 1788; on 23rd March, 1792, a report was made of the geological problems at the Colliery 'in the manor of East Coanwood', while a letter dated 20th September, 1820 contained an interesting summary of work carried out at Coanwood from 1760 onwards. The letter included estimates of the probable coal reserves in the area, and mentioned the desirability of employing a steam engine.

Confusingly, there were a cluster of separate mines in the vicinity of Coanwood station, the most important being Coanwood, East Coanwood and Featherstone. The pits were worked by different owners, but they tapped the same seams — thus, the 'Five Quarter' seam was worked by both Coanwood and Featherstone collieries, while this seam was also tapped by some of the local drift mines.

These mines were linked by a tramway which commenced at Coanwood (Herdley Bank) Colliery and ran more or less due east to Foster's Drift, where a short spur was provided. Beyond, the line continued across Moss House Lane, the gradient on this section being steep enough for the line to be worked as a self-acting inclined plane. There was a brake house at the bottom of the inclined section, and stables were sited at the top; a branch line diverged south-eastwards from the stables to reach Whalley Drift mine, and elderly residents can still remember 'long trains of horse-drawn wagons coming along to the top of the incline' before they were lowered down to Coanwood.

From the stables, the tramway maintained its easterly heading until, after crossing Christowell Burn, it curved sharply towards the south-east. Entering a short tunnel, it then passed under a minor road before climbing towards East Coanwood Colliery on another inclined plane. The line was single track throughout, the only double track sections being on the inclined planes.

The history of the tramway was inextricably linked with that of the surrounding collieries, and when East Coanwood pit was abandoned the line was apparently closed beyond Christowell (or Crystal-well); a drift mine was later driven at this point, allowing seams that had previously been worked at East Coanwood to be exploited by small-scale mining firms such as J. Ridley, who employed just 8 men at Crystal Well Drift around 1940. By that time, however, the tramway main line had long since fallen into disuse, though short sections were apparently retained in and around the mine.

Some Other Narrow Gauge Lines

The tramway between Featherstone Colliery and the nearby colliery sidings was a much simpler affair than its neighbour at Coanwood. Running more or less due east for half a mile, the Featherstone tramway was dead-straight, with no intermediate sidings. A similar line ran from the 'down sidings' at Alston to Newshield Quarry, but the Alston line was slightly more complex in that it passed under the Alston to Hexham road in a short tunnel, and branched out, at its eastern end, into a series of subsidiary tramways serving local lime quarries. Other lines served a battery of lime-kilns in which lime was burned prior to despatch by rail from Alston station.

The Alston tramway was worked in two parts, the upper portion between the quarries and the lime kilns, being worked by horse traction, while the section between the kilns and the main line was worked by gravity. The line was single throughout, with a passing place situated midway on the inclined section. The incline was worked by cable, the weight of descending vehicles being used to haul empties up to the kilns; the rate of descent was controlled by a band brake at the top of the incline.

The incline was still in use around 1920, though road vehicles were later used to convey lime from the kilns. Later still, the lime kilns were themselves abandoned, and the site of this once-busy quarry system has now reverted to nature, leaving the disused tramway as a monument to the days when lime formed an important source of outgoing traffic on the Alston branch.

Acknowledgements

Primary sources for this brief study were found in a variety of libraries and record repositories, some of the most important material being held in the University of Leicester library and the appropriate County Record Offices. At the same time, one must acknowledge the very great help provided by Alston residents and former railwaymen, and although it is insidious to single out individuals for special praise, the following people were especially forthcoming in terms of help, advice and anecdotal items: Arthur Middleton, Ken Hoole, J.B. Dawson, Alan Tweddle, Alan Robinson, Ruby Makepeace, S. Wright, George Kipling, Paul Lefevre, Peter Huntsman, T.H. Bell, W. Miller, J.A. Kent, Mrs F.M. Moone, David Bell, Laurie Ward, H.C. Casserley, E.E. Smith, K. Taylor, H.N. James, P.B. Booth, Mike MacDonald, J.W. Armstrong, G.B. Ellis, R.F. Roberts, J.E. Kite, Colin Judge, O.H. Prosser and Hazel Varty.

Further help came from the following organisations and individuals: British Rail, Lens of Sutton, The North of England Institute of Mining & Mechanical Engineers, The Historical Metallurgy Society, The British Geological Survey, The National Coal Board, Laurie Ward, and a multitude of Alston residents and former travellers, all of whom contributed in various ways. Apologies are due to those who have *not* been mentioned by name, the only defence for these omissions being the fact that the Alston project was initiated by one individual and completed by another — the result being that certain lines of research followed by the first author may not have been brought to a conclusion.

Appendix One

Population Figures

Population figures are of use to the railway historian, not only as an indication of the extent to which passenger traffic is likely to have been important to a given railway, but also as an indication of changing economic fortunes. In the latter case, the census figures for Alston are very revealing insofar as they reflect the growth of a lead mining community and its subsequent decline after the middle years of the 19th century. The figures quoted include Alston and the outlying hamlets of Nenthead and Garrigill.

Year	*Census Figure*		*Notes*
1801	4,746	(+)	
1811	5,078	(+)	
1821	5,699	(+)	
1831	6,858	(+)	
1841	6,062	(+)	
1851	6,815	(+)	Railway opened 17th November, 1852
1861	6,404	(−)	
1871	5,680	(−)	Decline of lead industry
1881	4,621	(−)	
1891	3,384	(−)	
1901	3,134	(−)	
1911	3,075	(−)	
1921	3,334	(+)	Birthrate up after World War I
1931	2,678	(−)	Onset of great depression
1951	2,327	(−)	
1961	2,105	(−)	
1971	1,909	(−)	

Class 'J39' 0–6–0 No. 64814 pauses for the camera at Alston on 24th August, 1954.
R.F. Roberts

Appendix Two

Facilities at Alston Station

Passenger platform (approx. 318 ft long)
Signal Box (approx. 17 ft × 13.5 ft)
Locomotive shed and workshops (approx. 85 ft × 19 ft)
Water tower with 7,000 gallon tank
Goods shed (approx. 70 ft × 40 ft)
Cattle pens
Weigh-house/office
Booking office/waiting rooms/parcels office
Sidings

	Length	'Standage'	Capacity
Goods shed siding	90 yds	64	12 wagons
Loading dock siding	116 yds	80	16 wagons
End-loading dock siding	63 yds	27	9 wagons
Cattle dock siding	150 yds	86	21 wagons
Alston Limestone siding	276 yds	199	39 wagons
Coal depot siding (1)	139 yds	92	19 wagons
Coal depot siding (2)	139 yds	92	19 wagons
Back siding	123 yds	75	17 wagons
Down siding (1)	232 yds	137	33 wagons
Down siding (2)	231 yds	136	33 wagons
Down siding (3)	288 yds	183	41 wagons
Down siding (4)	355 yds	263	50 wagons
Run-round loop	91 yds	83	13 wagons
Locomotive shed siding	156 yds	110	22 wagons
Carriage siding	65 yds	26	9 wagons

Turntable (42 ft 4 in. diameter) c.1878
Coal drops (16 × 12.25 ton cells)
Locomotive coaling stage
Water column
4-ton yard crane (originally 3-ton)

No. 67315 on the Alston branch train seen here at Haltwhistle in August 1951. Note the unusual NER bracket signal. *Oakwood Collection*

Appendix Three

Facilities at Intermediate Stations (*c.*1923)

SLAGGYFORD

11 chain (242 yds) loop siding
3.70 chain passenger platform (approx. 250 ft)
Booking office/waiting rooms
Station master's dwelling house
Goods loading dock and warehouse
Cattle dock
Signal cabin (approx. 17 ft × 13.5 ft)
Coal shed
Coal drops
Weigh-house
PW hut
1 goods siding and 1 private siding

LAMBLEY

4.50 chain passenger platform (approx. 300 ft)
Booking office and waiting rooms
Station master's dwelling house
Signal cabin (approx. 17 ft × 13.5 ft)
Goods store and loading dock
Coal shed
Cattle loading dock (Lambley Fell Branch)
Coal depot (Lambley Fell Branch)
PW hut (Lambley Fell Branch)
Private sidings (Lambley Fell Branch)

COANWOOD

14 chain (308 yds) loop
3.70 chain passenger platform (approx. 250
Booking office/waiting room
Signal cabin (approx. 17 ft × 13.5 ft)
Coal depot
Loading dock
1 ton yard crane
Goods siding and private colliery siding

FEATHERSTONE PARK

3.89 chain passenger platform (approx. 260
10.49 chain loop siding
Booking office/waiting rooms
Station master's dwelling house
Signal cabin (approx. 17 ft × 13.5 ft)
Loading dock (90 ft long)
Coal drops
2 ton yard crane
Goods sidings
Goods store
Cattle loading dock

PLENMELLER COLLIERY HALT

1.53 chain passenger platform (approx. 100 ft)
Plenmeller Colliery Ground Frame (2 levers)
Private colliery sidings

N.B. *'Standage' and total wagon capacity of Alston goods yard*

The official lengths of each siding in Alston goods yard are shown, together with amended figures which the NER defined as 'standage'. Careful examination of official plans suggests that the latter figures related to the length (in yards) of each siding relative to the appropriate loading or unloading area. For example, the 150 yard long cattle dock siding served an 80 yard long cattle dock, the resulting 'standage' for wagons being 86. Similarly, the total length of the Alston Limestone siding was 276 yards including 20 yards of the adjoining goods shed road. However, only 199 yards were available for loading or unloading purposes, and the 'standage' was therefore just 199. It appears, then, that 'standage' gave the NER authorities a rule-of-thumb guide to loading areas and was not an indication of the total wagon capacity — though the maximum storage capacity of the yard could easily be obtained by dividing the combined length of each siding by 21 ft (i.e. the average length of a pre-grouping short wheelbase goods vehicle).

Bibliography

Those seeking further information on the history of Alston and its mining industry will find that much has been written on mining, but comparatively little has been published in terms of purely railway history. The following bibliography may be of interest to those seeking to pursue their own studies; most of the learned journals mentioned will be found in any convenient university library.

Paul W. Wilson, The Nent Force Level, *Transactions of the Cumberland & Westmorland Antiquarian & Archaeological Society (New Series)* Vol. LXIII, 1963.

W. Wallace, *Alston Moor . . . its Mines & Miners* (1890).

J.D. Marshall & Michael Davies-Shiel, *Industrial Archaeology of the Lake Counties* (1969).

Mike Fenton, South Tynedale Railway, *Railway Magazine* December 1974.

Ken Hoole, *North Eastern Branch Line Termini* (1985).

Alan Harris, The Tindale Fell Waggonway, *Transactions of the Cumberland & Westmorland Antiquarian & Archaeological Society*, LXXII, 1972.

F.M. Trotter, The Alston Block, *Geological Magazine*, LXV, 1928.

D.J. Rowe, Occupations in Northumberland & Durham, 1851–1911, *Northern History*, VIII, 1973.

George Raw, Notes on the Overhead Koepe Winding Plant at Plenmeller Colliery, Haltwhistle, Northumberland, *Transactions of the Institute of Mining Engineers*, LV, 1917–18.

Alan Harris, Colliery Settlements in East Cumberland, *Transactions of the Cumberland & Westmorland Antiquarian & Archaeological Society (New Series)* LXXIV, 1974.

A.E. Smailes, The Lead Dales of the Northern Pennines, *Geography*, XXI, 1936.

G. Whittle, *The Newcastle & Carlisle Railway*.

Michael J. Denholm, Newcastle & Carlisle 150, *Railway Magazine*, CXXXI, 1985. March 1985.

W.W. Smyth, *Iron Ores of Great Britain* (1856).

R.C. Dunham, *The Geology of the Northern Pennine Ore Field* (1948).

J.N. Charters, *The Brampton Railway*.

Thomas Bell, *A Handbook of Slaggyford and the South Tynedale District* (1911).

Tom Bell, Rails Return to the South Tyne Valley, *Railway Magazine* May 1988.

Index